EXTRADITION LAW

(A COMPARATIVE ANALYSIS OF INDIA, USA AND EUROPE)

DR. ANIL KUMAR DIXIT

(M.A. in Political Science, LL.M., PGDJ and Ph.D.)
Professor & Principal, Career College of Law
Bhopal, (M.P)

TRUE SIGN
PUBLISHING HOUSE

Published by True Sign Publishing House
Address: 21, 2nd Floor, Kundan Nagar, Bagmugaliya,
Bhopal, Madhya Pradesh - 462026
E-mail: truesignbooks@gmail.com
Website: www.truesign.in

Extradition Law
(A Comparative Analysis Of India, Usa And Europe)

Dr. Anil Kumar Dixit

Edited By - Aashi Dixit (BBA LL.B)

ISBN: 978-93-5988-967-2

First Edition: 2023

ACKNOWLEDGEMENT

Writing a book is a journey that involves the support and contributions of many individuals. I am deeply grateful to those who have played a pivotal role in bringing this work to fruition.

First and foremost, I extend my heartfelt gratitude to my mother Late Mrs Brajrani Dixit, my father Late Mr. Vijay Krishna Dixit and my wife Late Mrs Shikha Dixit; your belief in me has always been my greatest source of motivation.

I would like to express my sincere appreciation to my mentors and advisors, whose guidance and insights have been invaluable. Your wisdom has shaped this book in ways I could not have accomplished alone.

A special thanks to my daughter Aashi Dixit (BBA LL.B.) who provided valuable feedback and encouragement throughout this endeavour. Your perspectives and encouragement have been instrumental in refining the ideas presented in these pages.

I am indebted to the readers who engage with this work. Your curiosity and interest in the subject matter inspire me to continue exploring and sharing knowledge.

Finally, I want to express my gratitude to the countless individuals who may not be mentioned by name but have, in various ways, contributed to the development of this book. Your collective influence has left an indelible mark on these pages.

Thank you, one and all, for being a part of this literary journey.

(Author)

PREFACE

In the ever-expanding realm of international law, the contours of extradition serve as a vital bridge between sovereign nations in the pursuit of justice. As we witness a world that grows smaller through increased connectivity, the complexities inherent in extradition processes become more pronounced and demand a comprehensive examination.

This book, "Extradition Law: A Comparative Analysis of India, USA, and Europe," is an exploration into the intricate tapestry of extradition frameworks, with a specific focus on three distinctive jurisdictions—India, the United States, and Europe. Each with its unique legal traditions, these regions present an intriguing panorama through which we delve into the convergences and divergences that shape contemporary extradition practices.

The objective of this comparative analysis is twofold: to provide a lucid understanding of the fundamental principles underpinning extradition law and to dissect the specific nuances that characterize the approaches of India, the USA, and Europe. As we traverse through historical developments, landmark cases, and legislative intricacies, the aim is to offer readers, be they legal practitioners, scholars, or policymakers, a nuanced insight into the functioning of extradition law in a global context.

The comparative lens applied in this study seeks not only to highlight the legal intricacies but also to unravel the practical implications of extradition decisions in diverse legal landscapes. In doing so, it is my aspiration that this book serves as a valuable resource for those navigating the complexities of cross-border justice.

I extend my sincere appreciation to the scholars, practitioners, and experts whose work has laid the groundwork for this comparative analysis. Their contributions have been instrumental in shaping the content of this book. Additionally, I express my gratitude to friends, colleagues, and family members whose unwavering support has been a source of motivation throughout this scholarly endeavor.

As we embark on this intellectual journey, may the pages that follow provide readers with a deeper understanding of the dynamic interplay between extradition law, national interests, and the pursuit of justice in an interconnected world.

Dr. Anil Kumar Dixit

Dated- 01st, December 2023

LIST OF ABBREVIATIONS

ABBREVIATIONS	EXPANSIONS
&	And
AIR	All India Reporter
CBI	Central Bureau of Investigation
CG	Central Government
Ch	Chapter
Ed.	Edition
EU	European Union
i.e	That is
IPC	Indian Penal Code
No.	Number
Ors.	Others
Para	Paragraph
Pg	Page
SC	Supreme Court
SCC	Supreme Court Cases
SLP	Special Leave Petition
TADA	Terrorist and Disruptive Activities (Prevention) Act
UAPA	Unlawful Activities Prevention Act
UK	United Kingdom
UPCS	Uttar Pradesh Civil Service
U.S	United States of America
v.	Versus
Vol	Volume

CONTENTS

INTRODUCTION

International extradition is the surrender by one nation to another, for trial and punishment, of a person accused or convicted of an offence within the jurisdiction of the latter[1]. A request for extradition is generally initiated against a fugitive criminal[2], who is formally accused of, or is charged with, or is convicted of an extradition sentence.

Extradition is a system consisting of several processes whereby one sovereign, surrenders to another sovereign, an individual sought after as an accused, criminal or fugitive offender. This delivery of individuals to the requesting sovereign is based on treaties and/or bilateral arrangements; however, sometimes this delivery of individuals occurs by reciprocity and comity as a matter of courtesy and goodwill between the sovereigns. World public order is the recurring theme based on which extradition is practiced by the States.[3] But it is always gainful to remember the observations made in the case of: ***U.S. v. Rauscher***[4]:

—*... Apart from them (treaties)... there was no well defined obligation on one country to deliver up such fugitives to another... and it has never been recognised as among those obligations of one government towards another which rest upon established principles of international law.*‖

In ***Oppenheim's International Law***, the expression **extradition** has been defined as follows:

---

[1] See: P. Ramanatha Aiyar‟s Concise Law Dictionary, Lexis Nexis, Fifth Edition, p.476

[2] A ‗fugitive criminal' means a person who is accused of, or is convicted of, an extradition offence within the jurisdiction of a foreign State and includes a person who, while in India, conspires or attempts to commit or incites or participates as an accomplice in the commission of an extradition offence in a foreign State.

[3] See: Abu Salem Abdul Qayyum Ansari v. CBI & Another, (2013) 7 SCR 1061.

[4] 119 U.S. 407 (at p.411 - 412).

—Extradition is the delivery of an accused or a convicted individual to the State where he/she is accused of or has been convicted of a crime, by the State on whose territory he/she happens for the time to be.‖ According to **Black's Law Dictionary**[5], extradition means: *—The surrender by one State or Country to another of an individual accused or convicted of an offence outside its own territory and within the territorial jurisdiction of the other, which, being competent to try and punish him,* demands the surrender.‖ Thus, in nutshell, extradition may be defined as: the act of sending, by authority of law, a person accused of a crime to a foreign jurisdiction where the crime was committed, in order that he may be tried there.

J.G. Starke in his work of acclaim, **Introduction to International Law** (10th Edition) defined the term extradition as follows: *—The term„ extradition" denotes the process whereby under a concluded treaty one State surrenders to any other State at its request, a person accused or convicted of a criminal offence committed against the laws of the requesting State, such requesting State being competent to try the alleged offender. Though extradition is granted in implementation of the international commitments of the State, the procedure to be followed by the courts in deciding, whether extradition should be granted and on what terms, is determined by the municipal law of the land."* Thus, extradition is founded on the broad principle albeit that, it is in the interest of civilised communities that criminals should not go unpunished and on that account it is recognised as a part of the comity of nations that one State should ordinarily afford to another State assistance towards bringing offenders to justice.[6] The Supreme Court of India, in the case of, **State of West Bengal v. Jugal Kishore**[7], defined extradition as the surrender by one State to another of a person desired to be dealt with for crimes of which he has been accused or convicted and which are justiciable in the courts of the other State.

---

[5]   See: Black's Law Dictionary, Centennial Edition (1891-1991), Sixth Edition, p. 585

[6]   See: Rosiline George v. Union of India, (1994) 2 SCC 80, Para 16; In this case, the Apex Court held that, the term _Extradition' denotes the process whereby under a concluded treaty one State surrenders to any other Stateat its request, a person accused or convicted of a criminal offence committed against the laws of the requesting State, such requesting State being competent to try the alleged offender.

[7]   AIR 1969 SC 1171.

Law relating to extradition in India is governed by: the Extradition Act, 1962[8] and the Extradition Treaties obtaining between India and other countries. By virtue of Section 34 of the 1962 Act, the Extradition Act of 1962 has extra-territorial jurisdiction, that is, an extradition offence committed by any person in a Foreign State shall be deemed to have been committed in India and such person shall be liable to be prosecuted in India for such offence. As per Section 216 of the Indian Penal Code, 1860 read with the Constitution of India, 1950 (Schedule VII, List I, Item 18), extradition may be defined as, the action of giving up a fugitive criminal to the authorities of the State in which the crime was committed. Extradition treaty means, a treaty, agreement or arrangement with a Foreign State relating to the extradition of fugitive criminals.[9] Treaty State means, a Foreign State with which an extradition treaty is in operation.[10] Section 3(4) of the 1962 Act categorically states that, where there is no extradition treaty made by India with any Foreign State, the Central Government may, by notified order[11], treat any Convention to which India and a Foreign State are parties, as an extradition treaty made by India with that Foreign State providing for extradition in respect of the offences specified in that Convention. As per Section 2(f) of the Extradition Act, 1962, only fugitive criminals, may be extradited. Fugitive criminal, as per the extradition law prevailing in India means: a person who is accused (or is convicted) of an extradition offence committed within the jurisdiction of a Foreign State, and a person who while in India, conspires, attempts to commit, incites or participates as an accomplice in the commission of an extradition offence in a Foreign State. As per Section 2(c) of the Extradition Act, 1962, an extradition

---

[8]   The Preamble of the 1962 Act describes it as follows: —An Act to consolidate and amend the law relating to the extradition of fugitive criminals and to provide for matters connected therewith or incidental thereto.

[9]   As per Section 2(c) (i) of the 1962 Act, an extradition treaty is a treaty between two or more nations which provides for the extradition from each of the countries to any of the others, of persons charged with specified offences.

[10]   As per Section 2(d) of the 1962 Act, an extradition treaty means a treaty or agreement made by India with a Foreign State relating to the extradition of fugitive criminals; and includes any treaty agreement or arrangement relating to the extradition of fugitive criminals made before the 15th day of August, 1947 which extends to, andis binding on, India.

[11]   See: Section 2(j) of the 1962 Act.

offence means, an offence provided in the extradition treaty with Foreign States; an offence punishable with imprisonment for a term which shall **not be less than one-year under the laws prevailing in India or of a Foreign State.** Section 2(a) of the 1962 Act defines a composite offence as, an act or conduct of a person occurring wholly or in part in a Foreign State or in India, effect of which (or intended effect which) taken as a whole would constitute an extradition offence in India or in a Foreign State,as the case may be.

In the case of ***Daya Singh Lahoria v. Union of India***[12], Supreme Court of India, expatiating over the importance of extradition law, stated the following, in authoritative terms:

Extradition is a great step towards international cooperation in the suppression of crime. It is for this reason that the Congress of Comparative Law at Hague in 1932, resolved that States should treat extradition as an obligation resulting from the international solidarity in the fight against crime.

PRINCIPLES ALBEIT THE LAW OF EXTRADITION:

a.   Principle Of Double Criminality:

This principle (also known as _Dual Criminality) states that, extradition is available only when the act in question is an offence in the jurisdictions of both the States (the requesting State and the State requested). The rationale behind this principle is that, the requested State should be at liberty to refuse to extradite the fugitive offender if they do not view the conduct of the fugitive offender as a criminal act.

b.   Principle of Specialty:

An extradited individual can be tried only for offences specified in the extradition request; the object of this principle is to prevent blanket extradition requests. The requesting State pledges to judge the requested person only for the crime for which extradition was requested, and not for any other offence.[13] As matter of fact, post the

---

[12]   2001 (4) SCC 516.

[13]   In Para 3 of the judgment, in the case of Daya Singh Lahoria v. Union of India, (2001) 4 SCC 516, the ApexCourt stated as follows: —A fugitive criminal brought into this country under an extradition decree can be tried only for the offences mentioned in the extradition decree and for no other offence and the criminal courts of this country will have no jurisdiction to try such fugitive for any other offence.‖

surrender of a fugitive offender, he/she can expressly waive the rule of speciality, and can be tried for offences in addition to, or in furtherance of the offences qua which he/she was surrendered. Moreover, in certain cases, the requested State can agree to the fugitive offender being tried for other offences, in addition to offences apropos which the fugitive offender was surrendered to the requesting State.

c. **Political Exception:**

Request albeit extradition must be declined if the real purpose of the request made is to punish the person requested for his political opinion rather than for the crime committed by him. Political offences exception holds that a person cannot be extradited for an offence of political character. The term political offences has not been clearly defined in international law. What shall construe as a political offence, usually, depends on the domestic law of the requested State. It is generally accepted that, acts of terrorism do not fall under the exception of political offences, even if they are committed with political motive.

PROCEDURE OF EXTRADITION: GENERAL:

- Extradition is governed by international treaties, bilateral or multilateral, enshrining the principle, nulla extradition sine lege (no extradition without a law), this principleis in fact a version of nullum crimine nulla pena sine lege (no crime and no penalty without a law).

- The State seeking the surrender of a person must present a formal extradition request, which must identify the wanted person and the offence imputed on him/her. The requesting State is required to submit certain documents in support of the request. Thekind and format of the evidence required, so also the standard of proof applied by the requested State may differ

---

In the case of Abu Salem Abdul Qayoom Ansari v. State of Maharashtra, (2011) 11 SCC 214, the Apex Court held that, the doctrine of speciality is a universally recognised principle of international law and partakes of doctrines of both, double criminality and reciprocity. Section 21 of the 1962 Act incorporates rule of specialityof the international law, it is for this reason that Section 21(a) mentions that extradited person cannot be tried foroffences other than those for which he was surrendered by a Foreign State. It was further held that, the rule of speciality is not violated when the extradited person is tried as also, for _lesser offences' as provided in Section 21(b) of the 1962 Act.

significantly from one country to another. The formal extradition request may be preceded by a provisional arrest warrant.

- Principle of comity of nations captivates that, each Member State must comply with a request from a court or prosecutor of another Member State for the execution of an arrest warrant issued by it against an individual accused of an offence carrying a minimum sentence of 12 months of imprisonment.

- The arrest warrant needs to contain only a description of the circumstances albeit which the offence was committed.

- The judicial authorities and not the executive, is to decide upon the request of extradition.

- Certain acts, that is, military, political or fiscal offences, have been deemed traditionally outside the realm of extraditable offences. Recent developments have added to this list the political offence exemption.

INDIA:

- A requisition for the surrender of a fugitive criminal is to be made to the Central Government by: (a) A diplomatic representation by the Foreign State, at Delhi; **or,** (b)The Government of the concerned Foreign State may communicate with the Central Government through its diplomatic representation in that State; **or,** (c) By other modes settled by arrangements ensuing between India and other countries.

- Upon requisition, the Central Government may, if it thinks fit, can order for an inquiry by a Magistrate. Magistrate for the purpose of Section 5 of the 1962 Act, shall mean: (a) A Magistrate of First Class or Presidency Magistrate (Section 2(g) of the 1962 Act); and (b) The Magistrate, who would have jurisdiction to enquire into the offence if it had been an offence committed within the local limits of his jurisdiction.[14]

---

[14] Section 5 of the 1962 Act- Order for Magisterial Inquiry: Where such requisition is made, the Central Government may, if it thinks fit, issue an order to any Magistrate who would have had jurisdiction to inquire into the offence if it had been an offence committed within the local limits of his jurisdiction, directing him to inquire into the case.

- On receipt of an order under Section 5 of the 1962 Act, the Magistrate shall issue a warrant for arrest of the fugitive criminal.[15]

- On appearance of the fugitive criminal before the Magistrate- the Magistrate shall: (a) Enquire into the case; (b) Take evidence in support of the requisition; (c) Takeevidence on behalf of the fugitive criminal including- evidence that no extradition offence is committed.

- Evidence before the Magistrate: In any proceeding against a Fugitive Criminal, exhibits, disposition (whether received or taken in the presence of the person against whom they are used or not), official certificates of facts and judicial documents (if duly authenticated), may be received in evidence before the Magistrate.[16]

- What may be termed as duly _authenticated documents: Warrants; the depositions orstatements on oath and copies thereof; certificates of, or judicial documents stating thefact of, a conviction- signed or certified under the hand of a judge, magistrate or officer of the State or by the official seal of a Minister of the State.

- If a prima-facie case is made out in support of the requisition- the Magistrate may commit the fugitive criminal to prison; shall report the result of inquiry to Central Government; shall forward the written submission, if any, filed by the fugitive criminal to the Central Government for consideration.

- If a prima-facie case is not made out in support of the requisition, then, Magistrate shall discharge the fugitive criminal.

- Surrender of fugitive criminal to the Foreign State: Upon satisfaction qua the prima- facie report of the Magistrate, the fugitive criminal may be surrendered to the Foreign State.

---

[15]   See: Section 6 of the 1962 Act.

[16]   See: Section 10 (1) of the 1962 Act.

RELIEF OF BAIL:

As per Section 25 of the 1962 Act (Release of Persons arrested on bail)-

a. In case of arrest or detention of a fugitive criminal under the 1962 Act, the provisions of the Criminal Procedure Code, 1973 relating to bail shall be applicable;

b. Magistrate shall have the same powers and jurisdiction as a Court of Session under the Code of Criminal Procedure, 1973; (c) Option of anticipatory bail, as well as, regular bail is available to the accused fugitive criminal.

- Restrictions on surrender of fugitive criminal: A fugitive criminal shall not be surrendered or returned if, the offence is political in nature[17]; the prosecution of offence is barred by time in the Foreign State; if the person is accused of any offence in India, other than the offence for which extradition is sought, or is

---

[17] Following offences are regarded as offences of political character albeit Section 31(2) of the 1962 Act: (a) Offences under the Anti-Hijacking Act, 1982; (b) Offences under the Suppression of Unlawful Acts against Safety of Civil Aviation Act, 1982; (c) An offence within the scope of the Convention on the punishment of crimes against Internationally protected persons including diplomatic agents, opened for signature at New York on 14.12.1973; (d) An offence within the scope of the International Convention against the taking of hostages opened for signature at New York on 18.12.1979; (e) Culpable Homicide and Murder (Sections 299 to 304, Indian Penal Code of 1860); (f) Voluntarily causing hurt or grievous hurt by a dangerous weapon or means (Sections 321 to 333, the Indian Penal Code of 1860); (g) Offences under the Explosive Substances Act, 1908;

(h) Possession of a fire-arm or ammunition with intention to endanger life (Section 27 of the Arms Act, 1959);

(i) Use of fire-arm with intention to resist or prevent the arrest or detention (Section 28 of the Arms Act, 1959);

(j) Causing of loss or damage to property used for public utilities or otherwise with intention to endanger life (Section 425 read with Section 440 of the Indian Penal Code of 1860); (k) Wrongful restraint and wrongful confinement (Sections 339 to 348 of the Indian Penal Code of 1860); (l) Kidnapping and abduction including taking of hostages (Sections 360 to 364A, the Indian Penal Code of 1860); (m) Offences related to terrorism andterrorist acts (The Terrorist and Disruptive Activities (Prevention) Act, 1987); (n) Abetting, conspiring or attempting to commit, inciting, participating as an accomplice in the commission of any of the offences listed above.

undergoing sentence under any conviction in India until after he has been discharged, whether by acquittal or on expiration of his sentence or otherwise; and until the expiration of 15 days from the date of his being committed to prison by the Magistrate.[18]

- Prosecution on refusal to extradition: Where the Central Government is of the opinion that a fugitive criminal cannot be surrendered or returned, pursuant to request for extradition by the Foreign State, the Central Government, if it deems fit and proper, it can take steps to prosecute such fugitive criminal in India.[19]

- Provisional Arrest under Section 34B of the 1962 Act: Upon urgent request from the Foreign State, the Central Government may request the Magistrate (having competent jurisdiction) to issue an immediate provisional warrant for the arrest of the fugitive criminal. It is necessary to mention that, the fugitive criminal is to be released upon the expiration of 60 days if no request qua his surrender or return is received, within the period of 60 days.

- Punishment of life imprisonment albeit an offence, punishment for which, ordinarily in India, is death penalty: Section 34C of the 1962 Act provides that, where a fugitive criminal has committed an extradition offence punishable with death penalty in India, is surrendered or is returned by the Foreign State on request of the Central Government (India); and the laws of the Foreign State do not provide for death penalty qua the offence for which the fugitive criminal is convicted, then the fugitive criminal shall be liable for the punishment of life imprisonment qua the offence.

- Appellate Remedies: (a) There is no provision of statutory appeal vis-à- vis extradition proceedings in the 1962 Act; (b) For redress of any grievance against any order vis-à- vis extradition proceedings, the writ jurisdiction of the High-Court concerned has to be invoked.

  Note: As of 31.07.2015, CBI (Central Bureau of Investigation) issued 650 red-corner notices pressing upon accused individuals

---

[18]　See: Section 31 of the 1962 Act.

[19]　See: Section 34A of the 1962 Act.

to face prosecution and serve penal sentences. Of the total 650 notices issued, 192 individuals were charged under laws that provide for death penalty as punishment, under the following legislation, the Arms Act, 1959[20]; the Indian Penal Code of 1860[21], the Maharashtra Control of Organized Crimes Act, 1999[22], the Narcotic Drugs and Psychotropic Substances Act, 1985[23], the Unlawful Activities Prevention Act, 1967[24], the Terrorist and Disruptive Activities (Prevention) Act, 1987[25], and the Prevention of Terrorism Act, 2002[26].

IMPORTANT CASE-LAWS:

1. *Dr. Babu Ram Saksena v. The State,* AIR 1950 SC 155: In the year 1869, the British Government and the State of Tonk entered into a treaty which provided for the extradition of offenders in respect of certain offences specified therein- called heinous offences, which did not include per se offences albeit cheating and extortion. In the

---

[20] Section 27(3) of the Arms Act, 1959; Section 27(3) was struck down by the Supreme Court in the case of State of Punjab v. Dalbir Singh, AIR 2012 SC 1040. It was held that, Section 27(3) of the 1959 Act imposed a mandatory death penalty. It was observed that, Section 27(3) of the 1959 Act was very wide in sense that anything done in contravention of Section 7 of the 1959 Act (which prohibited acquisition, possession, manufacture and sale of prohibited arms and ammunitions) was to be meted out with death penalty. It was observed that, under Section 302 of the Indian Penal Code, 1860, death penalty was not mandatory but was optional; the word _murder' is defined very elaborately under Section 300 of the Indian Penal Code, 1860 with various exceptions and explanations, but under Section 27(3) of the 1959 Act, there was imposition of mandatory death penalty without reasonable guidelines, setting the course albeit when death penalty should be attracted; Section 27(3) of the 1959 Act was observed to be devoid of exceptions, and was thus construed to be arbitrary. Section 27(3) of the 1959 Act was declared to be unconstitutional.

[21] Death Penalty under the Indian Penal Code of 1860 is provided for offences committed under the following Sections: 121, 132, 194, 195A, 302, 305, 307(2), 364A, 396, 376E and 376A.

[22] Section 3(1)(i) of the Maharashtra Control of Organized Crimes Act, 1999.

[23] Section 31A of the Narcotic Drugs and Psychotropic Substances Act, 1985

[24] Section 16(1) of the Unlawful Activities Prevention Act, 1967.

[25] Section 3(2)(i) of the Terrorist and Disruptive Activities (Prevention) Act, 1987.

[26] Section 3(2) (a) of the Prevention of Terrorism Act, 2002.

year 1903, the Indian Extradition Act came into effect; the 1903 Act provided for extradition in respect of cases albeit cheating and extortion, however, Section 18[27] of 1903 Act, provided that nothing contained in the 1903 Act shall derogate from the provisions of any treaty for extradition of offenders. Under the Independence of India Act, 1947, the suzerainty of His Majesty over the Indian States lapsed, and with it all treaties and arrangements in force; but under a stand-still agreement, between the Indian Dominion and the States (including the State of Tonk)all agreements between His Majesty and the States were continued, including agreements apropos extradition. State of Tonk acceded to the Dominion of India in 1947 and became a Member State of the United State of Rajasthan. The appellant in this case was a member of UPCS (Uttar Pradesh Civil Service) and his services were lent to the State of Tonk in 1948. After the appellant reverted to Uttar Pradesh, he was charged with offences of cheating and extortion, alleged to have been committed by him while he was in the State of Tonk and was arrested under an extradition warrant issued under Section 7 [28] of the 1903 Act. The appellant applied under

---

[27] Chapter 3 of the 1903 Act- Surrender of Fugitive Criminals in case of States other than Foreign States;Section 18 of the 1903 Act: Chapter not to derogate from treaties- Nothing in this Chapter shall derogatefrom the provisions of any treaty for the extradition of offenders, and the procedure provided by any such treaty shall be followed in any case to which it applies, and the provisions of this Act shall be modified accordingly.

[28] Section 7 of the 1903 Act: Issue of warrant by Political Agents in certain cases.— (1) Where an extraditionoffence has been committed or is supposed to have been committed by a person, 1[* * *] 2[in a Part B State orin the territories of any State outside India not being a Foreign State], and such person escapes into or is in 3[the territories to which this Act extends], and the Political Agent in or for such State issues a warrant, addressed to the District Magistrate of any district in which such person is believed to be, 4[or if such person is believed to bein any presidency-town to the Chief Presidency Magistrate of such town,] for his arrest and delivery at a place and to a person or authority indicated in the warrant, such Magistrate shall act in pursuance of such warrant and may give directions accordingly. (2)Execution of such warrant.—A warrant issued as mentioned in sub-section (1) shall be executed in the manner provided by the law for the time being in force with reference to the execution of warrants, and the accused person, when arrested, shall 5[be produced before the District Magistrate or Chief Presidency Magistrate, as the case may be, who shall record any statement made by him; such accused person shall then], unless released in accordance with the provisions of this Act, be forwarded to the place and delivered to the person or authority indicated in the warrant.

Sections 491 (Power to issue directions of the nature of a habeas corpus) and 561-A (Saving of inherent power of High Court Division) of the Code of Criminal Procedure, 1898, for his release, contending that, in view of the provisions of Section18 of the 1903 Act and the Extradition Treaty, 1869, appellant's arrest was illegal.

As per, H.J. Kania, Patanjali Sastri and Fazl Ali, JJ.:

It was held that, even assuming that the Extradition Treaty, 1869 subsisted after the merger of the State of Tonk inthe United State of Rajasthan; by providing for extradition for additional offences, the 1903 Act did not derogate from the 1869 Treaty or the rights of Indian citizens there under, and the arrest and surrender of the appellant under Section 7 of the 1903 Act was not unlawful qua the 1869 Treaty.

As per, B.K. Mukherjea, Fazl Ali, M.C. Mahajan and S.K. Das, JJ.:

It was held that, the Extradition Treaty, 1869 was not capable of being given effect to in view of the merger of the State of Tonk in the United State of Rajasthan, and, as no enforceable treaty right existed, Section 18 of the 1903 Act had no application; and so far as the conditions of Section 7 of the 1903 Act had been complied with, the warrant of arrest issued under Section 7 of the 1903 Act was not illegal.

2.   *The State of Madras v. C.G. Menon,* AIR 1954 SC 517: In this case it was held that, the scheme of the Fugitive Offenders Act, 1881, classifies fugitive offenders indifferent categories and then prescribes a procedure for dealing with each class. A comparison between the

---

(3) Proclamation and attachment in case of persons absconding.—The provisions of the Code of Criminal Procedure for the time being in force in relation to proclamation and attachment in the case of personsabsconding shall, with any necessary modifications, apply where any warrant has been received by a District Magistrate 6[or Chief Presidency Magistrate] under this section as if the warrant had been issued by himself.

1   The words —not being a European British subject‖ omitted by Act 17 of 1949, Section 5. 2 Substituted by the A.O. 1950 for —in the territories of any State not being a Foreign State‖ 3 Substituted by the A.O. 1950 for —the Provinces‖.

4   Inserted by Act 1 of 1913, Section 2.

5   Inserted by Act 1 of 1913, Section 2.

provisions of Part I (Return of Fugitives) and Part II (Inter- Colonial Backing of Warrants, and Offences) of the 1881 Act makes it clear that withregard to offences relating to which Part I has application, a fugitive when apprehended could not be committed to prison and surrendered unless the magistrate was satisfied that on the evidence produced before him there was a strong probable case against him, while with regards to a fugitive governed by Part II of the Act it was not necessary to arrive at such a finding before surrendering him. There was thusa substantial and material difference in procedure of surrendering fugitive offenders prescribed by the two parts of the 1881 Act.

Regarding persons committing offences in the United Kingdom and British Dominions and foreign countries in which the Crown exercised foreign jurisdiction, the procedure prescribed by Part I of the Act was to be followed before surrendering them and unless a prima facie case was established against them they could not be extradited. Extradition with foreign States is, except in exceptional cases, governedby treaties or arrangement made inter-se. Extradition of offenders between the United Kingdom and the Native States in India is governed by the Indian Extradition Act. Under the provisions of the Act no person apprehended could be surrendered unless aprima facie case was made out against him. After the achievement of independence and coming into force of the Constitution of India, 1950, India became a Sovereign- Democratic-Republic, and is no more a British Possession within the meaning of Section 12 of the Fugitive Offenders Act, 1881. India became a foreign country, post independence, so far as other British Possessions were concerned and the extradition of persons taking asylum in India, having committed offences in British Possessions could now only be dealt with by an arrangement ensuing between the Republic of India and the British

Government, and given effect to by an appropriate legislation.

The Indian Extradition Act, 1903 was adapted under the provisions of Article 372 of the Constitution of India, 1950. The 1903 Act did not keep alive any of the provisions of the Fugitive Offenders Act, 1881, which was an Act of British Parliament and which was not adopted post independence, and therefore, Section 12 and Section 14 of the Fugitive Offenders Act, 1881 does not applies to India.

3. ***Hans Muller of Nurenburg v. Superintendent, Presidency Jail, Calcutta and Ors.***, AIR 1955 SC 367: It was held that in India the Foreigners Act, 1946 confers the power to expel foreigners from India. It vests the Central Government with absolute and unfettered discretion and, as there is no provision fettering this discretion in the Constitution of India, 1950, an unrestricted right to expel remains. The law of extradition is quite different, because of treaty obligations it confers a right on certaincountries (not all) to ask that persons who are alleged to have committed certain specified offences in their territories, or who are alleged to have committed certain specified offences in their territories, or who have already been convicted of those offences by their courts, be handed over to them in custody for prosecution or punishment. But despite that the Government of India is not bound to comply withthe request and has an absolute and unfettered discretion to refuse.

It was further held that, there are important differences between the two Acts. Firstly, the Extradition Act applies to everybody, citizen and foreigner alike, and to every class of foreigner, that is to say, even to foreigners who are not nationals of the country asking for extradition. But, because of Article 19 of the Constitution of India,1950, no citizen can be expelled (as opposed to extradition) in the absence of a specific law to that effect; and there is none; also, the kind of law touching expulsion (as opposed to extradition) that could be made in the case of a citizen would have to be restricted in scope. That is not the case where a foreigner is concerned because Article 19 does not apply. But a citizen who has committed certain kinds of offences abroad can be extradited if the formalities prescribed by the Extradition Act are observed. A foreigner has no such right and he can be expelled without any formality beyond the making of an order by the Central Government. But if he is extradited instead of being expelled, then the formalities of the Extradition Act must be complied with. The importance of the distinction will be realised from what follows; and that applies to citizen and foreigner alike.

It was observed that, the Extradition Act is really a special branch of the law of criminal procedure. It deals with criminals and those accused of certain crimes. The Foreigners Act is not directly concerned with criminals or crime though the fact that a foreigner has committed offences, or is suspected of that, may be a good ground forregarding him as undesirable. Therefore, under the Extradition Act warrants or a summons must be issued; there must be a magisterial enquiry and when there is an arrest it is penal in character; and – this is most important distinction of all- when the person to be extradited leaves India he does not leave the country as a free man; he remains under arrest throughout and is merely handed over by one set of police to thenext.

4.   *In Re: K.R.P.L. Chockalingam Chettiar,* AIR 1960 Mad 548: In this case, the Full Bench of the Madras High Court, after referring to various authorities observed that, extradition is the delivery on the part of one State to another of those whom it is desired to deal with for crimes of which they have been accused or convicted and are justiciable in the courts of other State. Referring to 25 Corpus Juris, page 254, it was observed that, extradition has been defined to be surrender by one State or nation to another of an individual accused or convicted of an offence outside its own territory, and within the territorial jurisdiction of the other, which, being competent to try and punish him, demands the surrender. It was observed that, extradition must be distinguished from transportation and from deportation, which also results in the removal of a person from the country. Further it was noted that:

- *In re Arton,* (1896) 1 QB 108, it was held that, the foundation of extradition, which is the delivery on the part of one State to another of those who have fled from justice, is founded on the principle that the reciprocal surrender of criminals is in common interest of civilised communities.

- The objects of the Indian Extradition Act are as follows: (a) to provide for the more convenient administration of the Extradition Acts, 1870 and 1873, andof the Fugitive Offenders Act, 1881; (b) to amend the law relating to the extradition of criminals in cases to which the Extradition Acts, 1870 and 1873do not apply.

5.   *Rajender Kumar Jain & Ors v. State through Special Police Establishment & Ors,* 1980 (3) SCC 435: In this case the Apex Court observed that, politics are about Government and therefore, a political offence is one committed with the object of changing the Government of a State or inducing it to change its policy. To say that anoffence is of a political character is not to absolve, the offenders of the offence. But it will be a valid ground for the Government to advice the Public

Prosecutor to withdraw from the prosecution. The public prosecutor may withdraw from the prosecution of a case not merely on the ground of paucity of evidence but also in order to further the broad ends of public justice and such broad ends of public justice may well include appropriate social, economic and political purposes. It was further held that, the Indian Penal Code and the Code of Criminal Procedure do not recognise offences of political nature, as a category of offences; they cannot, in the ordinary course of things. That does not mean the offences of a political character areunknown to jurisprudence or that judges must exhibit such naiveté as to feign ignorance about them. International law recognises offences of political character andthe Indian Extradition Act specifically refers to them.

6.   ***Kubic Darusz v. Union of India,*** 1990 (1) SCC 568: Explaining the difference between preventive detention and extradition, the Apex *Court held as follows in this case-—Preventive detention of a foreign national who is not resident of the country involves an element of international law and human rights and appropriate authorities ought not to be seen to have been oblivious of its international obligationsin this regard.... The system of extradition of criminals represents an act of legal assistance by one State (the requestee) to another State (the requestor) with the aim of carrying out a criminal prosecution, finding and arresting a suspected criminal in order to bring him to court or for executing the sentence. In concluding such convention the States base themselves on principles of humanitarianism in their efforts to contribute to the more effective achievement of the objectives of the correction and re-education of violators of the law.*

Where such conventions exist, the citizens of a State who were convicted to deprivation of freedom in another signatory State are in accordance with mutual agreement of the States, transferred to the country of which they are citizens to serve their sentences. The transfer of the convicted person may take place only after the verdict has entered into legal force and may be carried out on the initiative of either of the interested States. The punishment decided upon with regard to a convicted person is served on the basis of the verdict of the State in which he was convicted. Onthe strength of that verdict the competent court of the State of which the person is a citizen adopts a decision concerning its implementation and determines, inaccordance with the law of its own State, the same period of deprivation of freedom as was assigned under the verdict. While such ameliorative practices may be available in case of a foreign national being criminally prosecuted, tried and punished, no such proceedings are perhaps possible when he is preventively detained.

A preventive detention as was held in Rex v. Halliday, 1917 AC 268, "is not punitivebut precautionary measure"… There may, therefore, be cases where while a citizen and resident of the country deserves preventive detention apart from criminalprosecution, in case of a foreign national not resident of the country he may not bejustifiably subjected to preventive detention in the event of which no international legal assistance is possible unlike in case of criminal prosecution and punishment.‖ In this case, taking note of the facts and circumstances albeit the case, the ApexCourt held that, ―*the continued detention of the detenu has been rendered illegal by non-consideration of his representation by the appropriate Government according to law resulting in violation of Article 22(5) of the Constitution; and he is to be set atliberty forthwith in this case.*

7.   *Sarabjit Rick Singh v. Union of India,* 2008 (2) SCC 417: In this case, taking note of the particular facts and circumstances of the case, the Apex Court observed as follows: ―*In a proceeding for extradition no witness is examined for establishing an allegation made in the requisition of the foreign State. The meaning of the word "evidence" has to be considered keeping in view the tenor of the Act. No formal trial is to be held. Only a report is required to be made. The Act for the aforementioned purposes only confers jurisdiction and powers on the Magistrate which he could haveexercised for the purpose of making an order of commitment. Although not very relevant, we may observe that in the Code of Criminal Procedure, 1973, the powersof the committing Magistrate has greatly been reduced. He is now required to look into the entire case through a very narrow hole. Even the power of discharge in the Magistrate at that stage has been taken away.*

8.   *Bhavesh Jayanti Lakhani v. State of Maharashtra,* (2009) 9 SCC 551: In this case itwas held that, fundamental rights of a citizen, whenever infringed, the High Court having regard to its extraordinary power under Article 226 of the Constitution, asalso keeping in view that access to justice is a human right, would not turn the citizenaway only because a red-corner-notice.[29] has been issued qua him by the

---

[29]   Red Corner Notice is issued by the Interpol to seek the provisional arrest of a wanted person. It by itself does not have the effect of warrant of arrest. It is issued for persons, against whom a national or international court has issued a warrant of arrest.

Interpol. Thesuperior courts in criminal cases are entitled to delve into the matter albeit themanner in which the red-corner-notice is sought to be enforced and/or whether the local police threatening an Indian citizen with arrest, is doing so without been legally entitled to do so, as except in terms of the 1962 Act.

9.   *Mohammed Zubair Fauzal Awam v. State (Represented by the Inspector of Police & Another)*, 2011 Cri LJ 2975: In this case, the Petitioner, a Sri-Lankan Tamilian temporarily residing in India, claimed that he had been staying in India with due permission from the authorities concerned. On strength of a red-alert-notice issued byInterpol (New Delhi), in pursuance of an arrest warrant that was issued by a competent court at Sri-Lanka, a case was registered under Section 41(1)

(g) of the Code of Criminal Procedure, 1973 against the petitioner. The Court, in this case, observed that, the consequence of a red-corner-notice is that the requesting State maymake a deportation request or may take a follow-up action with regards to the arrestof the petitioner, but since formal request was still to be made by the Sri-Lankan Government for extradition of the petitioner, arrest of the petitioner and registrationof FIR (First Information Report) under Section 41(1) (g) of the Criminal Procedure Code, 1973 qua him, was not proper.

10.   *P. Pushpavathy v. Ministry of External Affairs*, 2013 Cri LJ 4420: In this case it was held that, if a fugitive criminal accused of an extradition offence is arrested pursuant to a legally issued warrant of arrest by Magistrate who was directed by the Government of India to hold necessary inquiry; then in such a case the detention ensuing cannot be termed as illegal or un-lawful. When detention is not illegal or unlawful then no case can be made out for issuance of a writ of *habeas corpus*.

CURRENT STATE OF EXTRADITION LAW AND PRACTICE

A. Legal Basis for Extraditing

Under international law, there is no general duty to extradite[30]. Rather, extradition is understood to be a matter of international comity – that is, a favour accorded by one nation to another –, and the conditions under which an extradition request may be granted, or refused, are determined by the law of the requested State. Many States have enacted specific extradition laws and/or provisions on extradition in legislation on criminal procedure or penal codes, which enable States to extradite a fugitive to another State if requested. A legal obligation to extradite exists only where States have entered into bilateral or multilateral extradition agreements, or if they have become parties to international instruments which institute a duty to extradite with respect to specific offences [31].

---

[30]   See M.C. Bassiouni, above at fn. 1, at pp. 3–4; G. Gilbert, Transnational Fugitive Offenders in International Law, Martinus Nijhoff Publishers, The Hague, Boston, London (1998), at p. 47; see also Parliament of the Commonwealth of Australia, Joint Standing Committee on Treaties, "Extradition – A Review of Australia's Law and Policy", Report No. 40 (2001), at para. 2.3.

Criminal Court: A Commentary, Oxford University Press, Oxford (2002), at pp. 1589– 1598.

[31]   Under the relevant Security Council resolutions, States also have an obligation to cooperate with the international criminal tribunals for the former Yugoslavia and for Rwanda, which includes a duty to arrest and surrender a suspect, if so requested. States Parties to the Rome Statute of the International Criminal Court have an obligation to cooperate with the latter. This, however, is not extradition in the strict sense, as it concerns relations between a State and an organ established under international law, rather than two States. On the difference between "transfer"

1. Bilateral extradition agreements

Bilateral agreements establishing a reciprocal duty to extradite have traditionally been the preferred legal instrument used by States in their extradition relations. A large number of such treaties were concluded during the late 19th and early 20th centuries, many of which are still in force. Bilateral treaties continue to provide the legal basis for extradition in many cases.[32] In some countries, national law requires the existence of an extradition treaty as a precondition for permitting the surrender of a fugitive to another State. This has long been the case, in particular, for countries in the common law tradition, and still applies in the United States of America, but also in some civil law countries such as Brazil, the Netherlands or Slovenia.

There is no rule of international law which prevents States from extraditing in the absence of a treaty.[33] In many States, national legislation provides for the possibility of extraditing without a pre-existing agreement. Sometimes, this is subject to the explicit condition of reciprocity.[34] A number of common law countries have recently amended their extradition laws to allow for the possibility

---

and "surrender" to an international criminal jurisdiction, on the one hand, and "extradition", on the other, see B. Swart, "General Problems", in: A. Cassese, P. Gaeta and J.R.W.D. Jones (eds.), The Rome Statute of the International Criminal Court: A Commentary, Oxford University Press, Oxford (2002), at pp. 1589– 1598.

[32] It has been noted that bilateral extradition treaties are easier to negotiate than multilateral agreements. They permit the contracting States to take into consideration any particular political or legal concerns that may be relevant between them. See, for example, "International cooperation and practical technical assistance for strengthening the rule of law: promoting the United Nations Crime Prevention and Criminal Justice Programme", Background paper for the workshop on extradition and international cooperation, prepared for the Ninth United Nations Congress on the Prevention of Crime and the Treatment of Offenders, ,Cairo, 29 April–8 May 1995, UN doc. A/CONF.169/8, 1 March 1995, at paras. 18–20 and 37–39. See also G. Gilbert, above at fn. 2, at pp. 9–10 and 33.

[33] See P. Malanczuk, Akehurst's Modern Introduction to International Law, 7th rev. edn., Routledge, London, New York (1997), at p. 117.

[34] This is the case, for example, in Austria (s. 3 of the Law on Extradition and Mutual Legal Assistance of 1979); Belgium (s. 1 of the Law on Extradition of 15 March 1874); former Yugoslav Republic of Macedonia (Article 29(3) of the Constitution); Germany (s. 5 of the Law on International Mutual Assistance in Criminal matters of 23 December 1982); Moldova (Article 17 of the Constitution, s.23(2) of the Aliens

of extradition without pre-existing extradition relations with the requesting State [35].

2. Multilateral treaties and conventions on extradition

In addition to bilateral treaties, an increasing number of multilateral extradition agreements and conventions establish a mutual duty for States parties to extradite under the conditions set out by the respective instrument.

In 1990, the UN General Assembly adopted a Model Treaty on Extradition[36], which, together with a Model Treaty on Mutual Assistance in Criminal Matters[37], is intended to be "used as a basis for international co-operation and national action against organised crime and terrorist crime"[38]. It is not binding, however, and as yet there is no universal general extradition convention. Despite a shared interest in effective extradition relations, States'

States have found it easier to reconcile their differences at a regional or sub-regional level, although in some instances, including in closely integrated regions such as Europe, consensus was achieved through provisions for opt-out clauses or the possibility of making reservations to certain provisions in regional extradition instruments. In addition to the European instruments, regional extradition instruments include the following:

Law and s. 13(2) of the Criminal Code); Peru (s. 3 of the Law No. 24.710 of 1987 on Extradition); Russian Federation (s. 362 of the Code of Criminal Procedure); Slovak Republic (s. 373 of the Code of Criminal Procedure); Switzerland (s. 8(1) of the Federal Law on International Legal Assistance in Criminal Matters establishes a general requirement of reciprocity, but s. 8(2) provides for a number of exceptions.

[35] For example, the United Kingdom (Extradition Act 1989) or Canada (Extradition Act 1999). Australia had introduced a change permitting extradition on an ad hoc basis already in 1966 (Extradition (Foreign States) Act 1966)

[36] General Assembly Resolution 45/116 of 14 December 1990, Annex.

[37] General Assembly Resolution 45/117 of 14 December 1990, Annex.

[38] Eighth United Nations Congress on the Prevention of Crime and the Treatment of Offenders, Havana.27 August–7 September 1990: report prepared by the Secretariat, at para. 245, cited in United Nations, International Review of Criminal Policy Nos. 45 and 46, 1995, at p. iv

- Montevideo Convention on Extradition (Inter-American) (1933)[39]

- Convention on Extradition of the League of Arab States (1952)[40]

- Convention on Extradition of the Organisation Africaine et Malgache (OCAM) (1961)

- Inter-American Convention on Extradition (1981)

- Convention on Legal Aid and Legal Relations in Civil, Family and Criminal Cases of the Commonwealth of Independent States (1993)[41]

- Economic Community of West African States (ECOWAS) Convention on Extradition (1994)[42]

- South African Development Community (SADC) Protocol on Extradition (2002)

In addition, States members of the Commonwealth are bound by the London Scheme for Extradition within the Commonwealth, formerly known as Commonwealth Scheme on the Rendition of Fugitive Offenders[43]. Though not formally a treaty, this instrument, which was adopted in 1966 and last amended in November 2002, is binding for Commonwealth countries and contains guidelines to be implemented in their Extradition laws and agreements[44].

Historically, extradition relations have been particularly close among European States, and a comparatively large number of extradition

---

[39] Earlier extradition conventions in the Americas include the Montevideo Convention of 1989, a Convention concluded in Mexico in 1902, the Bolivarian Convention adopted in Caracas in 1911, and the Bustamante Code of 1928. See M.C. Bassiouni, above at fn. 1, at p. 22.

[40] A supplementary agreement to this Convention was concluded in 1983. See G. Gilbert, above at fn. 2, at p. 35.

[41] Hereinafter referred to as Minsk Convention (1993).

[42] Hereinafter referred to as ECOWAS Convention (1994).

[43] The Scheme was given its new title at the Commonwealth Law Ministers' meeting at Kingstown, St Vincent and the Grenadines, 18–21 November 2002.

[44] Hereinafter referred to as London Scheme for Extradition (1966 and 2002). The text of this instrument, including the most recent amendments, can be found in Annex B to the Communique issued by the Commonwealth Law Ministers on 21 November 2002, following their meeting at Kingstown.

instruments have been adopted in this region. They include the following:

- European Convention on Extradition (1957)[45] and its additional protocols of 1975[46] and 1978[47], adopted under the auspices of the Council of Europe.

- Benelux Treaty concerning Extradition and Mutual Assistance in Criminal Matters (1962), concluded between Belgium, the Netherlands and Luxembourg[48]

- Nordic States Scheme on extradition (1962), concluded between Denmark, Finland, Iceland, Norway and Sweden

- Agreement between the 12 Member States of the European Communities on the simplification and modernisation of methods of transmitting extradition requests (1989)

- Title III, Chapter 4 of the Convention implementing the 1985 Schengen Agreement (Schengen Convention, 1990)

- Convention on Simplified Extradition Procedures between the Member States of the European Union (1995)

- Convention Relating to Extradition between Member States of the European Union (1996)[49]

---

[45] This Convention has been ratified by 42 members of the Council of Europe as well as Israel, Serbia and Montenegro, and South Africa. It constitutes the principal legal basis for extradition practice in Europe. For ratification information, see at http://conventions.coe.int/ Treaty/EN/searchsig.asp?NT=024&CM=&DF= (ETS No.: 024)

[46] This protocol excludes war crimes and crimes against humanity from the category of political offences. It also defines cases where extradition can be refused on the ground that the offender has already been brought to trial.

[47] This protocol supplements and replaces certain provisions of the European Convention on Extradition concerning fiscal offences, judgments in absentia, amnesty etc.

[48] As completed and modified by the Protocol of 11 May 1974.

[49] Both the 1995 and the 1996 EU Conventions have not yet entered into force, as France and Italy have not ratified them. Both Conventions do, however, apply between Member States which have made declarations to that effect. These are, for the 1995 Convention: Austria; Denmark; Finland; Germany; Luxembourg; the Netherlands; Spain; Sweden; and the United Kingdom. For the 1996 Convention: Austria; Belgium; Denmark; Finland; Germany; Luxembourg; the Netherlands; Spain; Sweden; and the United Kingdom. The text of these declarations can be found in Schedules 2, 4, 6 and 8 to the UK European Union Extradition Regulations, 25 February 2002, available at: http://

These instruments have created a complex web of regulations governing extradition within the European Union as well as between Member States of the latter and third States[50]. As of 1 January 2004, the extradition regime under the above-listed instruments will be replaced within the European Union by a new system of mutually recognised and enforceable arrest warrants, as provided for in the Council Framework Decision of 13 June 2002 on a European Arrest Warrant and the Surrender Procedures between Member States.[51]

Extradition obligations under other international instruments

With regard to certain offences, the legal basis for extradition can be found in international law. This is the case, in particular, with regard to war crimes and certain crimes against humanity, acts considered to be terrorism and other types of transnational crime. Some of the international conventions concerned with the suppression, prevention and punishment of such crimes provide for an obligation to extradite for States Parties. Others enable States to extradite, rather than establishing a duty to do so. Customary international law may also serve as the basis for extradition without previous treaty arrangements.

---

www.hmso.gov.uk/cgi-

[50]   It has been noted that, as a result, it is often difficult to determine the exact conditions and requirements which apply to any given case. See, for example, S. Gleß, Auslieferungsrecht der Schengen- Vertragsstaaten, Neuere Entwicklungen, Projektbericht, Max-Planck-Institut für ausländisches und internationales Strafrecht, Freiburg im Breisgau, August 2002, available at: http://www.iuscrim.mpg.de/forsch/straf/projekte/gless.html, at p.8.

[51]   OJ L 190, 18.7.2002, pp. 1–18. The extradition instruments which will be superseded by the European arrest warrant will continue to apply in extradition relations between member States of the European Union and third States.

[52]   Crimes against humanity are defined in customary international law as serious crimes (such as, for example, murder, extermination, enslavement, torture, rape and other grave acts of sexual violence, the enforced disappearance of persons), when committed as part of an attack directed against a civilian population which is either widespread, or systematic, or both. 'Widespread' refers to the scale of the crime and means that it must involve a substantial number of victims. An attack is 'systematic' if it is part of a larger plan or pattern, usually involving a high degree of orchestration

a.   Crimes against humanity and war crimes

Crimes against humanity[52] and war crimes[53] are criminal offences under international law. The prohibition of such crimes imposes upon States obligations owed to the international community as a whole (erga omnes). It has also become part of jus cogens, that is, norms which protect fundamental principles and rank higher than treaty law and even general customary rules not endowed with the same force. One of the consequences of the jus cogens character of the prohibition of international crimes is that every State is entitled to investigate, prosecute, punish or extradite individuals accused thereof.[54] The fundamental character of the prohibition of war crimes and crimes against humanity also means that certain traditionally accepted grounds for the refusal to extradite will not apply in cases where extradition is requested for such crimes[55]. It does not, however, establish a general duty, based on customary law, to extradite in the absence of a treaty.[56]

An obligation to extradite those accused or convicted of certain international crimes is specifically provided for in some of the international instruments dealing with such acts:

---

and planning. But one single act can constitute a crime against humanity, if it is particularly egregious, or if it is committed as part of such a plan or pattern. Genocide, apartheid and torture, as defined in the relevant international conventions, are special cases of crimes against humanity. Crimes against humanity can be committed in times of armed conflict as well as times of peace.

[53]   War crimes are serious violations of international humanitarian law, committed in international and non-international conflict, as defined in international customary law and in treaties, such as, in particular, the four Geneva Conventions of 1949 and the two Additional Protocols thereto of 1977, as well as the relevant provisions of the Rome Statute of the International Criminal Court of 1998.

[54]   See Pinochet Ugarte, re. [1999] 2 All ER 97, at 108–109; see also the judgment of the International Criminal Tribunal for the former Yugoslavia (ICTY) in Prosecutor v. Anto Furundzija, Trial Chamber II, 10 December 1998, IT-95-17/1-T, at para. 156.

[55]   This is the case, in particular, with regard to the political offence exemption. See below at para. 76.

[56]   See B. Swart, "Arrest and Surrender", in: A. Cassese et al (eds.), above at fn. 3, at pp. 1655- 1658, and at p. 1660, with further references.

- Pursuant to Article 7(2) of the Convention on the Prevention and Punishment of the Crime of Genocide (1948), States Parties undertake to extradite suspects to the authorities of the State on whose territory genocide was committed, or to a competent international criminal tribunal.

- Article XI(2) of the International Convention on the Suppression and Punishment of the Crime of Apartheid (1973) establishes a mutual duty to extradite for States Parties.

- Article III of the UN Convention on the Non-Applicability of Statutory Limitations to War Crimes and Crimes against Humanity (1968) imposes a duty on States Parties to adopt all necessary measures to make possible the extradition, in accordance with international law, of the persons within its scope.

Other international instruments permit States to decide whether or not to extradite, but if they refuse to do so, they are under the obligation to prosecute the person in their own courts. This is known as the principle aut dedere aut judicare ("extradite or prosecute"). On the basis of Article 7(1) of the 1984 United Nations Convention Against Torture (UNCAT), it applies to the States Parties to that Convention. It is also provided for in Article 14 of the Inter-American Convention to Prevent and Punish Torture (1985); Article VI of the Inter- American Convention on Forced Disappearance of Persons (1994); Article 9(2) of the International Convention against the Recruitment, Use, Financing and Training of Mercenaries (1989); and Article 10(4) of the Convention on the Safety of United Nations and Associated Personnel (1994).

With respect to war crimes in international armed conflict – that is, grave breaches of the four Geneva Conventions of 1949[57] and of Additional Protocol No. I thereto of 1977

---

[57] The 1949 Geneva Convention for the Amelioration of the Condition of the Wounded and Sick in Armed Forces in the Field (GC I); the 1949 Geneva Convention for the Amelioration of the Condition of Wounded, Sick and Shipwrecked Members of Armed Forces at Sea (GC II); the 1949 Geneva Convention relative to the Treatment of Prisoners of War (GC III); the 1949 Geneva Convention relative to the Protection of Civilian Persons in Time of War (GC IV).

–the primary duty of States is to prosecute the perpetrators and instigators of such crimes[58]. These instruments establish mandatory universal jurisdiction for any State Party over those who commit, or order the commission of, war crimes. Each State Party has an obligation to search for such persons and bring them to justice before its own courts, regardless of their nationality. It may also, if it prefers, and in accordance with its own legislation, hand such persons over for trial to another State Party provided the latter has made out a prima facie case against the suspected war criminal[59]. Article 88(2) of Additional Protocol No. I provides that States Parties shall co-operate in the matter of extradition and give due consideration to the request of the State in whose territory the alleged offence has occurred[60].

There is no specific provision establishing a duty to prosecute or extradite persons accused of war crimes committed in non-international armed conflicts, although the principle aut dedere aut judicare is provided for in Article 9 of the Draft Code of Crimes of the International Law Commission (1996) for certain war crimes committed in non- international armed conflict, including, in particular, violations of common Article 3 of the Geneva Conventions of 1949.

---

[58] Pursuant to Article 50 GC I, Article 51 GC II, Article 130 GC III and Article 147 GC IV, grave breaches are the following acts, if committed against persons or property protected by the respective Convention: wilful killing, torture or inhuman treatment, including biological experiments, wilfully causing great suffering or serious injury to body and health, and extensive destruction and appropriation of property, not justified by military necessity and carried out unlawfully and wantonly. In addition, grave breaches comprise, under Article 130 GC III, compelling a prisoner of war to serve in the forces of the hostile Power, or wilfully depriving a prisoner of war of the rights of fair and regular trial prescribed in this Convention; and under Article 147 GC IV, unlawful deportation or transfer or unlawful confinement of a protected person, compelling a protected person to serve in the forces of a hostile Power, or wilfully depriving a protected person of the rights or a fair and regular trial prescribed in GC IV, as well as the taking of hostages.

[59] Article 49(1) and (2) GC I; Article 50(1) and (2) GC II; Article 129(1) and (2) GC III; Article 146(1) GC IV; Article 85(1) of Additional Protocol No. I of 1977.

[60] A duty to prosecute or extradite also applies to States Parties to the Hague Convention for the Protection of Cultural Property in the Event of Armed Conflict (1954) and the Second Hague Protocol for the Protection of Cultural Property in the Event of Armed Conflict (1999).

b. Acts of "terrorism" and other transnational crimes

A number of anti-terrorism conventions also contain provisions which establish a duty to extradite or prosecute those responsible for offences designated as terrorist acts. These include the following:

- European Convention on the Suppression of Terrorism (1977)[61]

- South Asian Association for Regional Cooperation (SAARC Regional Convention on Suppression of Terrorism (1987)[62]

- Arab Convention on the Suppression of Terrorism (1998)[63]

- Convention of the Organization of the Islamic Conference on Combating International Terrorism (1999)[64]

- Organisation of African Unity (OAU) Convention on the Combating and Preventing of Terrorism (Algiers Convention) (1999)[65]

By contrast, the Inter-American Convention against Terrorism (2002) does not impose an obligation to extradite or prosecute, but refers to States' obligations under already existing international anti-terrorism instruments as well as under their domestic law.[66]

The principle aut dedere aut judicare also applies under the following international instruments dealing with the suppression and punishment of specific offences:

- Convention for the Suppression of Unlawful Seizure of Aircraft (1970)[67]

---

[61] Article 7.

[62] Article IV.

[63] Article 6(h). The obligation to prosecute in case of non-extradition only applies where extradition is precluded because the legal system of the requested State does not allow it to extradite its nationals.

[64] Article 6(8). The obligation to prosecute in case of non-extradition only applies where extradition is precluded because the legal system of the requested State does not allow it to extradite its nationals.

[65] Article 8(4).

[66] Article 9.

[67] Article 7.

- Convention for the Suppression of Unlawful Acts against the Safety of Civil Aviation (1971)[68]

- Convention on the Prevention and Punishment of Crimes against Internationally Protected Persons, including Diplomatic Agents (1973)[69]

- International Convention against the Taking of Hostages (1979);[70]

- Convention on the Physical Protection of Nuclear Material (1980)[71]

- Convention for the Suppression of Unlawful Acts against the Safety of Maritime Navigation (1988)[72]

- Protocol for the Suppression of Unlawful Acts against the Safety of Fixed Platforms Located on the Continental Shelf (1988)[73]

- International Convention for the Suppression of Terrorist Bombings (1997)[74]

- International Convention for the Suppression of the Financing of Terrorism (1999)[75]

A duty to extradite or prosecute also applies to the States Parties to the following international conventions dealing with other types of transnational crime:

- Single Convention on Narcotics Drugs (1961), as amended by the Protocol amending the Single Convention on Narcotics Drugs (1972)[76]

---

[68]   Article 7.

[69]   Article 7.

[70]   Article 8(1).

[71]   Article 10.

[72]   Article 6(4).

[73]   Article 3(4).

[74]   Article 8(1).

[75]   Article 10(1).

[76]   Article 36(2)(iv).

- United Nations Convention against Illicit Traffic in Narcotic Drugs and Psychotropic Substances (1988)[77]

- United Nations Convention against Transnational Organized Crime (2000)[78]

These conventions typically require States Parties to ensure that the acts in question are offences under their criminal law, coupled with an obligation to either extradite a person suspected of having committed such crimes or submit their cases to their own competent authorities for the purpose of prosecution. Many such instruments also contain provisions to the effect that the offences within their scope shall be deemed to be included as an extraditable offence in any existing bilateral treaties that apply between States Parties, as well as enabling States Parties to use them as surrogate extradition treaties in the absence of pre-existing bilateral extradition agreements. Where extradition is not conditional upon the existence of a treaty, these acts are to be considered extraditable offences under national law[79].

There are conflicting opinions as to whether the principle aut dedere aut judicare has become part of customary international law[80]. The predominant view continues to be that there is no such obligation[81].

---

[77] Article 6(9)(a).

[78] Article 16(10). The obligation to prosecute in case of non-extradition applies only where extradition is refused solely on the grounds that the person concerned is a national of the requested State, and at the request of the State seeking extradition.

[79] Such provisions are also contained, for example, in Article 8 of the United Nations UNCAT (1984), and Article 15 of the International Convention against the Recruitment, Use, Financing and Training of Mercenaries (1989).

[80] M.C. Bassiouni and E.M. Wise, Aut Dedere Aut Judicare: The Duty to Extradite or Prosecute in International Law, Martinus Nijhoff Publishers, Dordrecht, Boston, London (1995), at pp. 20–25;

M.C. Bassiouni, Crimes against Humanity in Criminal International Law, 2nd rev. edn., Martinus Nijhoff Publishers, Dordrecht, Boston, London (1999), at pp. 219–221, goes as far as to suggest that the principle of aut dedere aut judicare has become jus cogens where aggression, war crimes, genocide and other crimes against humanity are involved.

[81] See, for example, B. Swart, above at fn. 29, at pp. 1662-1663, who notes the absence of sufficient State practice and opinio juris in support of it as the main difficulty in supporting the argument that aut dedere aut judicare has become a norm of customary international law. G. Gilbert, above at fn. 2, states that "there is certainly no rule of customary international law that fugitives in general should be extradited or prosecuted", but that "a new norm of international law may be developing" (at p. 14).

4. Hierarchy of obligations

Most States are bound by extradition obligations arising from bilateral and multilateral extradition agreements as well as extradition provisions in other international instruments dealing with terrorism or other types of transnational crime. A significant number of such agreements may apply in any given country. For example, the United States of America is a party to over 100 bilateral or multilateral extradition treaties.[82] Similarly, the United Kingdom has extradition relations with more than 100 countries[83], while Australia has entered into more than 45 extradition agreements[84]. Canada, too, has concluded over 50 bilateral extradition treaties and is a party to several multilateral conventions. 42 European countries, as well as Israel, Serbia and Montenegro and South Africa, have ratified the European Convention on Extradition[85]. In addition, many European States have also concluded bilateral treaties with countries in Europe and elsewhere[86].

At the same time, States have obligations under international law which preclude them from granting extradition under certain circumstances. International human rights and refugee law, as well as customary international law, impose bars on extradition where fundamental rights of the individual concerned would be at risk.

As a consequence, a State which must determine a request for the extradition of a person within its jurisdiction may find itself in a conflict of obligations under various pertinent legal instruments. Such conflicts must be resolved in accordance with applicable principles and standards of international law.

Traditionally, extradition was seen as a matter between States as the only subjects of international law. The individual affected was considered to be a mere "object", without standing to assert

---

[82]   See A. Powers, "Justice Denied? The Adjudication of Extradition Applications", 37:277 Texas International Law Journal (2002), at p. 283.

[83]   See Extradition Procedures in the United Kingdom, Home Office, 2002, available at: http://www.homeoffice.gov.uk/oicd/jcu/extranote.htm.

[84]   Parliament of the Commonwealth of Australia, above at fn. 2, at para. 2.23.

[85]   For ratification information see above at fn. 18.

[86]   Belgium, for example, is party to 58 bilateral agreements. See I. Delbrouck, Guide de la personne, Supplément 18, December 2000, at p. 9.

violations of their individual rights as a result of extradition, except on the grounds that it would be contrary to specific provisions of the applicable inter- state agreement[87]. With regard to the current state of international human rights and refugee law, however, this view is no longer tenable.

a. Conflicting obligations nunder extradition agreements and conventions

In principle, international treaties between States have the same force under international law. This may give rise to conflicting obligations under different treaties. The requested State may have a duty to extradite under a bilateral or multilateral extradition agreement, but it may also have an obligation under another – usually regional – treaty to refuse extradition under certain circumstances.

A number of extradition conventions contain clauses which clarify their relationship with other conventions and/or bilateral treaties. Thus, for example, Article 28 of the European Convention on Extradition (1957) provides that its provisions supersede those of any bilateral treaties, conventions or agreements governing extradition between any two Contracting Parties. States Parties may conclude bilateral or multilateral agreements among themselves only to the extent that they supplement the Convention or facilitate its implementation[88]. Similar provisions are contained in Article 32 of the ECOWAS Convention (1984). Article 3 of the recent extradition agreement between the European Union and the United States of America determines for each of its clauses whether it is applicable in place of, in addition to, or in the absence of bilateral treaty provisions between EU Member States and the United States of America, which

---

[87]　See J. Dugard and C. van den Wyngaert, "Reconciling extradition with human rights", 92:2 American Journal of International Law (1998), 187, at pp. 188-190, with references to case law in the United States, Canada and the United Kingdom, which "interprets extradition laws and treaties in favour of enforcement because this course is perceived to serve the interests both of justice and of friendly international relations".

[88]　See Article 59 of the Schengen Convention (1990) and Article 1, respectively, of the 1995 and 1996 EU Conventions dealing with extradition (see above at para. 19). The European arrest warrant scheme suspends the extradition provisions of various European instruments (see above at para. 20).

the new treaty is intended to supplemen[89]. By contrast, Article 33 of the Inter-American Convention on Extradition (1981) provides that multilateral and bilateral treaties remain in force unless the States Parties concerned expressly declare or agree otherwise. However, such declarations cannot suspend the applicability of international human rights treaties.

Article 30 of the Vienna Convention on the Law of Treaties (1969) sets out general rules for the application of successive treaties between the same parties and on the same subject matter which do not contain explicit provisions as to which of them should take

precedence over the other. In brief, the later treaty will normally prevail over the earlier one, and the more specialised over the more general.

b.   Extradition obligations vs. obligations under other international treaties

The above-described rules do not apply to conflicts of obligations under treaties dealing with different subject matters, in particular human rights and refugee protection instruments. Such treaties create not merely subjective, reciprocal rights and duties between States, but rather "particular legal orders involving objective obligations to protect human rights".[90] With respect to those rights guaranteed under international human rights treaties which have attained the status of jus cogens, or peremptory norms of international law, Articles 53 and 64 of the Vienna Convention on the Law of Treaties (1969) apply and provide that any treaty provisions which conflict with jus cogens are void[91]. Thus, the prohibition of handing a person over to a country

---

[89]   Agreement on extradition between the European Union and the United States of America, signed on 25 June 2003, OJ l 181, 19.7.2003, pp. 27–32. The agreement is not yet in force.

[90]   See M.N. Shaw, International Law, 4th edn., Cambridge University Press, Cambridge (1997), at p. 696.

[91]   Article 53 of the Vienna Convention on the Law of Treaties provides: "A treaty is void if, at the time of its conclusion, it conflicts with a peremptory norm of general international law. For the purposes of the present Convention, a peremptory norm of general international law is a norm accepted and recognized by the international community of States as a whole as a norm from which no derogation is permitted

where he or she would be exposed to a risk of torture, cruel, inhuman or degrading treatment or punishment always prevails over an duty to extradite pursuant to an extradition treaty binding the requested and the requesting States[92]. The same holds for other fundamental rights which are recognised as forming part of jus cogens[93].

41. Conflicts arising from the requested State's duties under extradition agreements, on the one hand, and its obligations under international human rights or refugee instruments which do not constitute peremptory norms of international law, on the other, need to be resolved on the basis of States' obligations under the UN Charter.

Articles 55(c) and 56 of the UN Charter impose a duty on States to promote and respect human rights. Article 103 of the UN Charter provides that, "[i]n the event of a conflict between the obligations of the Members of the United Nations under the present Charter and their obligations under any other international agreement, their obligations under the present Charter shall prevail". Human rights bars to extradition therefore take precedence over a duty to extradite which may exist on the basis of an agreement between the requested and the requesting State.

c.   Extradition obligations vs. obligations under customary international law

Customary international law may also impose obligations on the requested State which take precedence over extradition agreements. Where the applicable norm of customary international law is a peremptory norm of international law, or jus cogens, the same considerations apply. As for other international law principles which have not (yet) attained such status, the relation between treaties and custom is more differentiated. As a general rule, the later in time will

---

and which can be modified only by a subsequent norm of general international law having the same character." Under Article 64 of the same Convention, "[i]f a new peremptory norm of general international law emerges, any existing treaty which is in conflict with that norm becomes void and terminates".

[92]   On the jus cogens character of the prohibition of exposing a person to a risk of torture, cruel, inhuman or degrading treatment or punishment.

[93]   The Human Rights Committee lists as examples of violations of peremptory norms of international law the taking of hostages, imposing collective punishments,

prevail[94]. Thus, where the requested State's duty to extradite under a treaty precedes the emergence of a new rule of customary international law which establishes a bar to extradition, it will be superseded by the latter. This may be the case in particular with regard to the principle of non- refoulement under customary international law. Once a new rule of customary international law has emerged, States are bound by it. Treaties concluded subsequently must be read in the light of existing obligations under customary international law.

---

arbitrary deprivations of liberty or deviating from fundamental principles of fair trial, including the presumption of innocence. See Human Rights Committee, General Comment No. 29 on States of Emergency (Article 4), 2001, UN doc.

CCPR/C/21/Rev.1/Add.11, at para. 11.

[94]   See M.N. Shaw.

UNITED STATES: INTERNATIONAL EXTRADITION: A GUIDE TO U.S. AND INTERNATIONAL PRACTICE

The U.S. government's efforts to extradite Julian Assange from the United Kingdom have prompted broad discussion of—and questions about—the law and practice of international extradition.[95] A decision in the Assange case is expected early next year.[96] Other recent well-publicized international extradition cases include those of Omar Ameen, an Iraqi refugee in the United States whom Iraq sought on what critics call a questionable murder charge.[97] Mullah Krekar, an Iraqi Kurdish cleric extradited from Norway to Italy following his conviction in Italy for leading a jihadist group[98]; and Emilio Lozoya, the former chief of the Mexican state oil firm Pemex, who was arrested in Spain earlier this year as Mexico prepared to seek his extradition on corruption charges.[99]

For each of these well-known cases handled by authorities around the world, however, U.S. diplomatic and law enforcement authorities deal with dozens of important but lower-profile requests for extradition—

---

[95] See William Booth, U-Md. professor testifies, amid glitches, at Assange extradition hearing in London, The Wash. Post (Sept. 7, 2020).

[96] See Mia Swart, Julian Assange extradition verdict to be delivered on January 4, Al Jazeera (Oct. 2, 2020).

[97] See Ben Taub, The Fight to Save an Innocent Refugee from Almost Certain Death, The New Yorker (Jan. 20, 2020).

[98] See Norway extradites jihadist preacher Mullah Krekar to Italy, BBC News (Mar. 26, 2020).

[99] See Spain orders detention of ex-head of Mexico oil firm pending extradition request, Reuters (Feb. 13, 2020).

both to and from the United States—as part of the regular work of international law enforcement cooperation.

The process by which the United States evaluates these incoming and potential outgoing extradition requests may be unfamiliar to some practitioners. This Advisory is meant to provide a basic primer for those interested in understanding the law and practice of international extradition, with a focus on the U.S. process. It first addresses the basic elements common to most bilateral extradition treaties. Next, it describes

the process for extradition to and from the United States. Finally, it discusses some of the defenses most commonly raised in extradition cases, along with suggestions for handling such matters to achieve the best results for individuals facing potential extradition.

GENERAL OVERVIEW OF EXTRADITION TREATIES

Extradition treaties are intended to operate like contracts and obligate the parties to arrest and surrender a person to a foreign treaty partner upon request, provided that the treaty's requirements are met and no exceptions apply. Extradition treaties are individually negotiated and may vary in order to accommodate the legal systems and priorities of the negotiating countries, but they generally share common elements. They establish requirements for both the country sending the extradition request (the "requesting state") and the country receiving the request (the "requested state").

The United States has extradition treaties with more than 100 countries.[100] U.S. extradition proceedings are also subject to the requirements of U.S. statutory law, most importantly those codified at 18 U.S.C. § 3181 et seq. In general, the United States will extradite an individual to another country only under the authority of a bilateral extradition treaty with that country[101], but it will accept fugitives from other countries whether based on a bilateral extradition treaty,

---

[100]   See U.S. Dep't of State, 7 Foreign Affairs Manual (FAM) 1613.1(c). The State Department compiles an annual publication titled Treaties in Force, which contains the most up-to-date list of countries with which the United States has extradition treaties. See U.S. Dep't of State, Treaties in Force (last accessed November 10, 2020).

[101]   Under U.S. statutory law, extradition generally is possible "only during the existence of any treaty of extradition with {the relevant} foreign government."

the provisions of a multilateral convention[102], or other means of return.[103]

EXTRADITABLE OFFENSES

All treaties include provisions defining which crimes are extraditable. Treaties agreed upon prior to the 1970s typically contain a negotiated list of specific extraditable offenses (such as "murder," "manslaughter," or "larceny") and permit extradition only for the crimes that are listed in the treaty. Modern treaties have largely done away with these lists, however, and use a "dual criminality" approach instead.[104] This more flexible approach examines the conduct that serves as the basis for the request.[105]

Exceptions to extradition

Every extradition treaty contains exceptions to the parties' extradition obligations. The most common exceptions include:

Political offenses.

These provisions are aimed at crimes such as treason, espionage, and other offenses that could be used to target political opponents or otherwise cause the requested state to become entangled in the domestic politics of the requesting state. To clarify and limit the contours of the "political offense" exception, most U.S. bilateral

---

18 U.S.C. § 3181(a). Section 3181(b) provides a narrow exception authorizing the surrender of persons other than U.S. citizens, nationals, or permanent residents who have committed crimes of violence against U.S. nationals abroad, provided that the Attorney General makes certain certifications in writing.

[102] Although the United States has entered into a number of multilateral conventions that provide for extradition, "{a}s a matter of practice, the United States does not extradite, based solely on a multilateral convention, to a state with which we have no bilateral treaty." 7 FAM 1613.3(d).

[103] See 7 FAM 1642.1 (discussing mechanisms by which the United States may seek the deportation or expulsion of a person from another country); U.S. Dep't of Justice, Justice Manual (JM) 9-15.610 (same).

[104] See 7 FAM 1613.3(c).

[105] See 7 FAM 1613.3(a) ("The principle of 'dual criminality' . . . reflects the internationally accepted understanding that a requested state will only extradite a person for prosecution or punishment if the alleged or proven conduct, had it occurred in the territory of the requested state, would also be deemed criminal.").

treaties now exempt violent conduct such as bombings and hostage-taking from the exception, even if the individual sought for extradition asserts that the conduct in question was political in nature.[106]

Nationality

Many countries refuse to extradite their own nationals, and where that position prevails in negotiations, an extradition treaty may include an exception for this policy. The U.S. government has long held the view

that nationality should not operate as a bar to extradition, since the requesting state should have the right to pursue criminal charges against persons who violate its laws regardless of nationality. The U.S. government accordingly extradites its nationals and seeks to limit nationality-based denials of its outgoing requests.[107] In addition, U.S. statutory law expressly permits the Secretary of State to surrender a U.S. citizen to a foreign country when the extradition judge has issued a certification of extraditability and "the other requirements of [the applicable] treaty or convention are met."[108]

Prior proceedings (non bis in idem)

These provisions, which appear in most extradition treaties, bar extradition where the person has already been convicted or acquitted in the requested state of the offense for which extradition is requested.[109]

---

[106]   See, e.g., Extradition Treaty, U.S.-U.K., art. 4(2), Mar. 31, 2003, S. Treaty Doc. No. 108-23 (listing specific offenses that "shall not be considered political offenses," including "a murder or other violent crime against the person of a Head of State of one of the Parties, or of a member of the Head of State's family," and "an offense involving kidnaping, abduction, or any form of unlawful detention, including the taking of a hostage"). Another common approach is found in the 1998 U.S.-Korea extradition treaty, which excludes from the "political offense" exception any "offense for which both Contracting States have the obligation to extradite the person sought or to submit the case to their competent authorities for decision as to prosecution pursuant to a multilateral international agreement." Extradition Treaty, U.S.-S. Kor., art. 4(1), June 9, 1998, S. Treaty Doc. No. 106-2.

[107]   See 7 FAM 1613.4(c) ("As a matter of policy, the United States no longer negotiates new extradition treaties if the partner country is unwilling or unable to commit to extradition of nationals.").

[108]   18 U.S.C. § 3196.

[109]   See 7 FAM 1613.4(a).

The concept is similar to the U.S. doctrine of "double jeopardy." Capital offenses.

Although the United States tries to limit the application of this exception in its bilateral extradition treaties, many treaties contain provisions permitting the requested state to demand assurances that the death penalty will not be sought or imposed.[110] For example, the U.S.-South Africa treaty provides that "when the offence for which extradition is sought is punishable by death under the laws in the Requesting State, and is not punishable by death under the laws in the Requested State, the Requested State may refuse extradition unless the Requesting State provides assurances that the death penalty will not be imposed, or if imposed, will not be carried out."[111]

Rule of specialty

The doctrine of specialty provides that "the requesting state may, after the fugitive has been surrendered to it, prosecute or punish the fugitive only for the crime or crimes for which extradition was granted, subject to certain exceptions."[112] A common modern formulation of this doctrine, as explained by the U.S. Senate Committee on Foreign Relations in its report on the U.S. extradition treaty with Cyprus, is that "a person extradited under the Treaty may only be detained, tried, or punished in the Requesting State for: (1) the offense for which extradition was granted or a differently denominated offense based on the same facts, provided the offense is extraditable or is a lesser included offense; (2) an offense committed after the extradition; or (3) an offense for which the executive authority of the Requested State consents."[113]

Procedural and documentation requirements

Extradition treaties generally contain provisions that specify the documents and information required to support an extradition request, along with any translation and authentication requirements. Typically,

---

[110]   See 7 FAM 1613.4(e).

[111]   Extradition Treaty, U.S.-S. Afr., art. 5, Sept. 16, 1999, S. Treaty Doc. No. 106-24

[112]   7 FAM 1612.

[113]   S. Exec. Rep. No. 105-23, at 66-67 (1998).

the requesting state must provide information about the identity of the person sought (including specific descriptive information); the text of relevant laws; information about the facts and procedural history of the case; documentation relating to the charges or convictions; and any other information the parties have deemed necessary to evaluate the request. With respect to requests for extradition for a person sought from the United States, U.S. extradition judges have interpreted U.S. extradition treaties and statutory law as requiring evidence sufficient to, at minimum, support a finding of "probable cause" that the person is guilty of the charges pending in the requested state.[114]

Statute of limitations

Because statutes of limitations for particular offenses vary by country, many treaties include provisions specifying which country's statute of limitations will apply or, in some cases, providing that the passage of time is no bar to extradition. U.S. extradition treaties typically provide that the statute of limitations in the requesting state should be the only relevant limit.

Extradition Process

The extradition process in the United States (and in most other countries) involves both executive officials and judges who preside over extradition proceedings. In the United States, executive-branch responsibility for overseeing the extradition process is shared by the Department of State's Office of the Legal Adviser (specifically the Office of Law Enforcement and Intelligence) and the Department of Justice's Office of International Affairs (OIA), with substantial assistance from federal prosecutors around the United States.[115] Extradition is proper only if an applicable extradition treaty is in place, all of its requirements are met, and none of its exceptions apply. Given the complexity and sensitivity of the issues involved, extradition is a time-consuming process, often taking years.

---

[114]   he U.S. Supreme Court has described this standard as requiring "competent evidence to justify holding the accused to await trial, and not to determine whether the evidence is sufficient to justify a conviction." Collins v. Loisel, 259 U.S. 309, 316 (1922).

[115]   See 7 FAM 1614.1(a), (c).

EXTRADITION FROM THE UNITED STATES

Step 1: The Department of State receives and conducts an initial review of the extradition request.

The process begins when the requesting state sends an extradition request to the State Department through diplomatic channels.[116] Upon receiving the request, the State Department determines whether (1) there is a treaty in force between the United States and the requesting state.

(2) whether the request appears to meet the requirements of that treaty.[117]

It also forwards the documents to OIA so that OIA can conduct its own review.[118] During this period, the State Department may ask the foreign government to clarify, supplement, or resubmit the request if the supporting documentation is incomplete or unclear.

Most modern extradition treaties allow the requesting state to seek "provisional arrest" of the subject while it prepares the formal request, which can reduce the possibility that a person will flee while the request is being finalized.[119] The specific terms under which provisional arrest is permitted and the length of time a person can be held until a full extradition request is transmitted vary from treaty to treaty.

Step 2: OIA conducts a parallel sufficiency evaluation.

OIA conducts its own review of the request to verify that the request is complete and that the documents establish probable cause to believe that subject committed the crime charged.[120] If the State Department

---

[116]   See 7 FAM 1616(a) ("The request is generally made as a diplomatic note with accompanying documents, by the government's embassy in Washington, D.C., to the Department (L/LEI)."); JM 9- 15.700 ("Foreign requests for extradition of fugitives located in the United States are ordinarily submitted by the embassy of the country making the request to the Department of State, which reviews and forwards them to the Criminal Division's Office of International Affairs (OIA).").

[117]   See 7 FAM 1616(b).

[118]   See 7 FAM 1616(b), 1634.1(a).

[119]   See 7 FAM 1616(f).

[120]   See 7 FAM 1634.1(c).

and OIA jointly decide to pursue the extradition request, the State Department will formally transmit the original request and supporting documents to OIA, along with a declaration attesting that the request meets certain applicable treaty requirements.[121]

Step 3: OIA forwards the request to an appropriate U.S. Attorney's Office, which then seeks an arrest warrant.

If the request survives this initial review, OIA forwards the relevant documents to the U.S. Attorney's Office in the district in which the subject is located with instructions on how to proceed.[122] That office assigns an Assistant United States Attorney (AUSA) to the case.[123] The AUSA then files the appropriate papers in U.S. district court.[124]

According to the State Department, the practice "varies by district": "some prosecutors will file the extradition request when applying for the arrest warrant," while "others will merely refer to the request in the affidavit accompanying the application for the warrant and submit the actual request at the extradition hearing."[125]

Step 4: Proceedings before the extradition judge.

The individual then appears before a U.S. magistrate or district court judge for proceedings, generally including an initial appearance, bail determination, and hearing under 18 U.S.C. § 3184 (often called the "probable cause" hearing). In connection with the probable cause hearing, the extradition judge determines whether: "(1) there is a treaty in force; (2) the person arrested is in fact the person sought by the requesting state; (3) the crime of which the fugitive is accused is an extraditable crime under the treaty; (4) the request sets out probable cause to believe that

---

[121]　See 7 FAM 1616(b), 1634.1(a)-(b); see also JM 9-15.700 ("The Department of State will separately verify in a transmission to OIA that there is a treaty in force between the United States and the country making the request, that the crime or crimes are extraditable offenses under the terms of the treaty, and that the supporting documents are properly certified.").

[122]　See JM 9-15.700; 7 FAM 1616(c).

[123]　See JM 9-15.700.

[124]　See id.

[125]　7 FAM 1634.1(d).

the fugitive committed the charged crime; and (4) there are no treaty grounds requiring denial of extradition[126]." The specific issues addressed during the hearing depend on the provisions of the treaty and any defenses to extradition available under the law. Importantly, the probable cause hearing is not a trial on the merits, and the rules of evidence and criminal procedure do not apply as they would at a criminal trial.[127] In general, individuals may offer "explanatory" evidence that provides an exculpatory explanation of the requesting state's evidence, but they are not generally permitted to offer evidence merely to contradict the evidence provided by the requesting state.[128]

Step 5: Certification by the extradition judge and decision by the Secretary of State.

If the extradition judge concludes that the request satisfies the probable cause standard and that the other requirements of the treaty are met, the judge will prepare a certification of extrudability and transmit the record of the case to the Secretary of State for a final decision on whether to order the extradition.[129] The State Department's Office of the Legal Adviser then conducts a detailed review of the case. The Department "considers any written materials submitted to the Secretary of the State by the fugitive, his or her counsel, family, or interested parties."[130] The Department also "will consider the likely treatment of the fugitive in the requesting country, including possible issues under the Convention Against Torture, as well as questions about political motivation."[131] The Secretary has ultimate discretion to determine whether the subject should be released or surrendered.[132]

---

[126]   7 FAM 1616(d); see also 7 FAM 1634.2(b).

[127]   See JM 9-15.700; 7 FAM 1634.2(a); see also, e.g., Skaftouros v. United States, 667 F.3d 144, 155 & n.16 (2d Cir. 2011).

[128]   See 7 FAM 1634.2(c).

[129]   See 18 U.S.C. § 3184; 7 FAM 1616(e), 1635.1(a); JM 9-15.700.

[130]   7 FAM 1635.1(b).

[131]   Id.

[132]   See 18 U.S.C. § 3186; United States v. Kin-Hong, 110 F.3d 103, 109 (1st Cir. 1997).

Certifications of extraditability are not directly appealable.[133] Rather, the sole avenue for challenge is a petition for writ of habeas corpus.[134] A court decision denying the petition may be appealed.[135]

Step 6: Notification and transit or release.

Once the Secretary of State decides whether an individual should be extradited, U.S. authorities will promptly notify the requesting state.[136] Where the Secretary has ordered the surrender of the person sought for extradition, OIA—in coordination with officials of the requesting state—will arrange for the person's transfer to that country.[137]

EXTRADITION PROCESS FOR THE UNITED STATES

Step 1: Federal, state, or local prosecutor forwards extradition request to OIA.

Requests for extradition are initiated by the prosecutor handling the potential prosecution in the United States and must be reviewed and approved by OIA before they are forwarded to the Department of State.[138]

Step 2: OIA conducts sufficiency review.

OIA is responsible in the first instance for reviewing possible outgoing extradition requests, ensuring that they are legally sufficient, and deciding whether to ask the State Department to make a formal extradition request through diplomatic channels. After receiving a request, OIA, consulting with the State Department as needed, confirms the following:

1. "an extradition treaty is in force between the United States and the recipient country";

---

[133]   See JM 9-15.700; 7 FAM 1634.2(f); see also, e.g., Ordinola v. Hackman, 478 F.3d 588, 598 (4th

Cir. 2007) (citing Collins v. Miller, 252 U.S. 364, 369 (1920)).

[134]   See JM 9-15.700; 7 FAM 1634.3(a).

[135]   See JM 9-15.700; 7 FAM 1634.3(c).

[136]   See JM 9-15.700, 7 FAM 1634.2(g).

[137]   See JM 9-15.700; 7 FAM 1614.2(b).

2. "both countries' legal systems recognize the fugitive's crimes as criminal (dual criminality) and extraditable";

3. "the fugitive is procedurally extraditable, considering elements such as the citizenship of the fugitive and types of evidence that are available to the U.S. prosecutor"; and

4. "the applicable statutes of limitations governing the crimes in both the United States and the other country have not expired."[139]

OIA attorneys are the Department of Justice's subject-matter experts on extradition, and federal, state, and local prosecutors are required to route requests through OIA rather than directly contacting their foreign counterparts.[140]

Step 3: OIA forwards the request to the Department of State.

If OIA determines that the request is sufficient, it forwards it to the Department of State for additional review.[141] Because all requests for extradition must be sent through diplomatic channels, the request will proceed only if the Department of State agrees it is sufficient.[142] If the request clears this second review, the Department of State will transmit an instruction to the appropriate overseas post.[143]

While the formal request for extradition is being prepared, the Justice Department may request the provisional arrest of the subject.[144] Depending on the provisions of the relevant extradition treaty, detention under a provisional arrest warrant may be limited to a specific time period,[145] such as 45 or 90 days. The person can be released if the United States does not submit a formal extradition request within the specified time period. Although a formal extradition

---

[139]   See JM 9-15.210; 7 FAM 1615(b).

[140]   See JM 9-15.210.

[141]   See 7 FAM 1615(b).

[142]   See id.

[143]   See id.

[144]   See 7 FAM 1615(e).

[145]   See 7 FAM 1612.

request must be transmitted to the requested state by the Department of State, some modern treaties permit OIA to transmit a request for provisional arrest directly to the requested state's Justice Ministry.[146]

Step 4: The Department of State forwards the request to the requested state for extradition proceedings.

The Department of State then sends the extradition documents to the U.S. embassy in the requested state, which will formally present them to the relevant ministry under cover of a diplomatic note.[147] After receiving the request, competent authorities of the requested state undertake their own review. Procedures vary by country, but many countries' processes entail a review similar to that in the United States, including executive approval and review by a judge. Extradition determinations may be subject to appeal and, as in the United States, proceedings may take months or years to complete.[148]

Step 5: Notification and transit or release (or other disposition).

Once the requested state reaches a decision regarding a U.S. extradition request, it will notify the U.S. government. If the request is denied, OIA may work with prosecutors and the Department of State to evaluate other options for obtaining custody of the individual, such as deportation.[149]

International Extradition: A Guide to the European Union and International Practice

In an increasingly interconnected world, transnational crime knows no borders. Criminals exploit this interconnectedness to evade justice by crossing into foreign territories. To counter this, countries engage

---

[146]　See JM 9-15.700.

[147]　See JM 9-15.700.

[148]　See id. ("Though factual defenses to extradition are limited, the fugitive may delay a decision hrough procedural challenges. The determination of extraditability is often subject to review or appeal. Prediction of the time required to return an individual to the United States is difficult and depends on the circumstances of the individual case and the practice of the foreign country involved.").

[149]　See JM 9-15.600-650.

in international extradition, a legal mechanism enabling the transfer of individuals to face prosecution or serve sentences in the jurisdiction where the crime was committed or charges are pending.

Extradition is akin to a diplomatic contract between nations, governed by bilateral and multilateral agreements. These treaties dictate the conditions under which a country may request and execute the surrender of an individual from another country.

The European Union (EU) has made significant strides in harmonizing extradition procedures among its member states, fostering a collaborative approach to combat cross-border crime.

Historically, extradition treaties listed specific offenses eligible for extradition. Modern treaties, including those within the EU, have adopted the 'dual criminality' principle, where the act in question must be considered criminal in both the requesting and requested states.

This shift allows for more flexibility in determining extraditable offenses, adapting to the evolving nature of criminal activities.The cornerstone of extradition within the EU is the European Arrest Warrant (EAW) system. Instituted to expedite the extradition process, the EAW system removes political and administrative obstacles, streamlining the transfer of individuals between member states. This has significantly enhanced the efficiency and speed of extradition procedures, fostering a cohesive approach to criminal justice within the EU.

This guide navigates through the intricacies of international extradition, focusing on the European Union's role and practices. It explores the legal foundations, procedural aspects, and key mechanisms, shedding light on how the EU facilitates the extradition process in alignment with international norms and evolving legal paradigms.

Extradition within the European Union

Extradition within the European Union (EU) represents a harmonized legal framework aiming to facilitate the swift surrender of individuals for prosecution or punishment across member states. The EU's approach to extradition has evolved significantly with the establishment of the European Arrest Warrant (EAW) system, streamlining processes and promoting a seamless legal cooperation.

This chapter explores the historical context, legal foundations, procedures, and key mechanisms that define extradition within the EU. [150]

Historical Evolution

Historically, extradition within Europe was complex and time-consuming, often hindered by diverse legal systems, procedures, and political considerations among member states. Each country had its extradition laws, leading to inconsistent practices and challenges in ensuring fugitives faced justice. Recognizing this impediment, the EU sought to harmonize extradition rules to enhance efficiency and collaboration in the fight against transnational crime.

Legal Foundations

The cornerstone of extradition within the EU is the European Arrest Warrant (EAW) system, implemented in 2004150. The EAW operates on the principle of mutual recognition, wherein member states recognize and enforce each other's judicial decisions, including arrest warrants. It simplifies extradition procedures, overcoming the need for dual criminality and streamlining the surrender of individuals. The EAW lists 32 offenses for which surrender is mandatory, without assessing the dual criminality of the act[151].

The European Arrest Warrant (EAW) System

The EAW system revolutionized extradition within the EU by removing political and administrative barriers[152]. It allows for the swift transfer of individuals accused or convicted of crimes

---

[150]   P. de Hert, "The European Arrest Warrant: A Critical Appraisal, Ten Years After," in M. Simonato et al. (eds.), The Area of Freedom, Security, and Justice in the Enlarged Europe (Brussels: Peter Lang, 2014), 251-266.

[151]   Council Framework Decision of 13 June 2002 on the European Arrest Warrant and the Surrender Procedures between Member States (2002/584/JHA).

[152]   D. Derlén and M. Edvardsson Björnberg, "The European Arrest Warrant and Its Relationship to Fundamental Rights," in A. Weyembergh et al. (eds.), The European Arrest Warrant in Practice (Cambridge: Intersentia, 2013), 25-46.

from one member state to another. Upon receiving an EAW, the requested state must execute the arrest and surrender of the individual within specified time frames. The surrender process is based on trust and mutual recognition, streamlining cooperation and ensuring a unified approach to criminal justice within the EU.[153]

Key Mechanisms

Framework Decision 2002/584/JHA

Framework Decision 2002/584/JHA established the EAW, setting out the legal framework and procedures for its implementation. It laid the foundation for mutual recognition of arrest warrants and surrender procedures, promoting cooperation and expediting extradition within the EU[154].

Surrender Procedures

Surrender procedures under the EAW system are efficient and well-defined. Member states must designate a central authority responsible for processing EAWs and overseeing the surrender process. The requested state's authorities, upon receipt of an EAW, must promptly locate, arrest, and surrender the individual to the requesting state. The process ensures a quick and effective response, promoting a harmonized approach to extradition within the EU.

Key Features of the European Arrest Warrant (EAW) System

The European Arrest Warrant (EAW) system, a foundational component of extradition within the European Union (EU), embodies key features that have revolutionized cross-border judicial cooperation and extradition processes within the EU. This section elucidates the fundamental characteristics that define the EAW system and its impact on streamlining extradition.

---

[153]   Council Framework Decision of 13 June 2002 on the European Arrest Warrant and the Surrender Procedures between Member States (2002/584/ JHA).

[154]   Council Framework Decision of 13 June 2002 on the European Arrest Warrant and the Surrender Procedures between Member States.

Simplified Extradition Procedures

The EAW system operates on the principle of mutual recognition, aiming to simplify and expedite extradition procedures.[155]

Traditional extradition processes, often rife with complexity, have been replaced by straightforward procedures, ensuring a swift response to extradition requests. By minimizing administrative burdens and eliminating political considerations, the EAW system promotes a seamless surrender process.

Abolition of Dual Criminality Requirement

A significant departure from traditional extradition norms, the EAW system abolishes the dual criminality requirement for 32 offenses listed in the Framework Decision. This departure ensures that extradition is automatic for these offenses, regardless of whether the act is considered a crime in the requested state. Such an approach enhances efficiency and expedites the extradition process.

Limitation of Grounds for Refusal

The EAW system significantly restricts the grounds on which a member state can refuse extradition[156]. The Framework Decision provides a limited set of grounds for refusal, focusing primarily on ensuring fundamental rights and preventing abuse of the system. By narrowing down the scope of refusal, the EAW system facilitates smoother collaboration among member states.

Strict Timeframes for Surrender

To ensure prompt response and adherence to the extradition process, the EAW system mandates strict timeframes for surrender. Member states are required to surrender the individual within a fixed timeframe, typically 10 to 60 days. This stringent requirement enhances efficiency and avoids unnecessary delays in extradition cases.

---

[155]   Treaty on European Union (TEU).

[156]   Treaty on the Functioning of the European Union (TFEU).

The Role of European Union Institutions

In the realm of extradition within the European Union (EU), the role of EU institutions is pivotal in ensuring a coherent and effective framework for cooperation among member states. This section delves into the significant role played by EU institutions in shaping and overseeing the extradition processes, harmonizing legislation, and fostering mutual trust.

European Commission

The European Commission acts as the main driving force behind EU-wide cooperation in the field of justice and home affairs, including extradition. It plays a crucial role in evaluating member states' compliance with the European Arrest Warrant (EAW) system, conducting assessments, and proposing improvements to ensure efficient functioning. Additionally, the Commission facilitates dialogue and information exchange among member states, fostering a culture of collaboration in the extradition domain.[157]

European Parliament

The European Parliament, representing the EU's citizens, actively participates in shaping legislation related to extradition and judicial cooperation. Through its powers of legislative initiative and consent, it influences the development of legal frameworks such as the EAW system, contributing to the establishment of uniform rules and procedures for extradition within the EU.[157]

Council of the European Union

The Council of the European Union, comprised of representatives from member states' governments, plays a central role in the legislative process for extradition matters. It adopts legislative acts and sets general EU policies regarding judicial cooperation, including extradition procedures and mechanisms.

The Council's decisions profoundly impact the extradition landscape within the EU, aiming for a harmonized and effective system.

---

[157] Treaty on the Functioning of the European Union (TFEU).

Court of Justice of the European Union (CJEU)

The CJEU interprets EU law and ensures its uniform application across all member states. In the realm of extradition, the CJEU provides authoritative interpretations of legal concepts and principles, resolving disputes and offering guidance to national courts. Its judgments play a significant role in shaping the extradition landscape and fostering legal certainty.

Extradition from the European Union

Extradition from the European Union (EU) involves a legal process through which individuals can be surrendered from EU member states to third-party countries for prosecution or punishment. This chapter provides a comprehensive overview of the legal framework and procedures governing extradition from the EU, emphasizing the key laws and principles that underpin this vital aspect of international cooperation.

Legal Framework for Extradition from the EU

Extradition from the EU is primarily governed by bilateral agreements between the EU and third-party countries, as well as international conventions.

Key legal instruments include:

The European Arrest Warrant (EAW) Framework Decision:

Enacted in 2002, this decision established the legal basis for the EAW system within the EU. It streamlines the extradition process for serious offenses within the EU, eliminating administrative and political barriers. The EAW Framework Decision sets out the grounds for refusal of surrender, rights of the person concerned, and procedures for surrender.[158]

---

[158] Council Framework Decision of 13 June 2002 on the European Arrest Warrant and the Surrender Procedures between Member States (2002/584/ JHA).

Bilateral Extradition Agreements:

EU member states often have bilateral agreements with third-party countries governing extradition. These agreements detail the offenses for which extradition can be requested and the procedures to be followed.

Key Features of the European Arrest Warrant (EAW) System

The EAW system revolutionized extradition within the EU, enhancing efficiency and speed. Some notable features include:

List of Offenses:

The EAW covers a wide range of offenses, including terrorism, murder, rape, and other serious crimes. The list of offenses is expansive, ensuring a comprehensive approach to extradition.

Surrender Procedure:

The requesting state issues an EAW to the requested state, which must execute the warrant without evaluating the evidence. The surrender procedure is swift, allowing for timely extradition.

Specialty Rule:

The EAW system upholds the principle of specialty, ensuring that individuals are only prosecuted or punished for the offenses specified in the EAW. Any additional offenses require consent from the requested state.

Dual Criminality Principle

The principle of dual criminality is fundamental in extradition cases, ensuring that the act for which extradition is sought is considered a crime in both the requesting and requested jurisdictions. This principle acts as a safeguard, preventing the extradition of individuals for actions that are not criminal in the requested state.

Extradition Procedures from the EU

The procedures for extradition from the EU to third-party countries are guided by the specific legal agreements in place. However, a common extradition process includes:

Extradition Request:

The requesting country submits a formal extradition request to the requested member state, providing necessary documentation and information.

Evaluation:

The requested member state evaluates the request, considering the legality and validity of the request, as well as the presence of dual criminality.

Judicial Review:

If the extradition request meets the legal criteria, it may undergo judicial review to ensure compliance with legal standards.

Human Rights Considerations

Extradition from the EU is conducted with due consideration for human rights. Member states and third-party countries must adhere to international human rights standards, including the prohibition of torture, inhumane or degrading treatment, and ensuring a fair trial[159].

Challenges and Considerations

Extradition from the EU presents challenges, including balancing the interests of justice, protecting individual rights,and navigating the complexities of international law. Overcoming these challenges necessitates a careful evaluation of legal frameworks and a commitment to upholding the rule of law.

Extradition to the European Union

Extradition to the European Union (EU) is a legal process that involves surrendering individuals from third-party countries to EU member states for prosecution or punishment. This chapter provides an in-depth exploration of the legal framework, procedures, and key laws governing extradition to the EU. It underscores the importance of international cooperation and adherence to legal principles in facilitating this essential aspect of transnational justice.

---

[159]   Universal Declaration of Human Rights, G.A. Res. 217A (III) (1948)

Legal Framework for Extradition to the EU

Extradition to the EU is primarily governed by bilateral agreements between third-party countries and the EU, as well as international conventions.

Key legal instruments include:-

Bilateral Extradition Agreements:

These agreements between third-party countries and the EU member states outline the offenses for which extradition can be requested and the procedures to be followed.

The European Arrest Warrant (EAW) Framework Decision:

Although primarily governing extradition within the EU, the EAW Framework Decision can also influence extradition to the EU by setting a standard for the surrender of individuals for serious offenses.

Legal Principles Governing Extradition to the EU

Several legal principles guide extradition to the EU, ensuring fairness and adherence to the rule of law:

Dual Criminality: Just like in extradition from the EU, the principle of dual criminality is fundamental in extradition to the EU, ensuring that the act for which extradition is sought is considered a crime in both the requesting and requested jurisdictions.

Human Rights Safeguards: Extradition to the EU must adhere to international human rights standards, including the prohibition of torture, inhumane or degrading treatment, and ensuring a fair trial.

Extradition Procedures to the EU

The procedures for extradition to the EU from third-party countries typically involve the following steps:

Extradition Request: The requesting country submits a formal extradition request to the EU member state, providing necessary documentation and information.

Evaluation: The EU member state evaluates the request, considering the legality and validity of the request, as well as the presence of dual criminality.

Judicial Review: If the extradition request meets the legal criteria, it may undergo judicial review to ensure compliance with legal standards.

The Role of EU Institutions

EU institutions play a crucial role in facilitating and coordinating extradition processes. Institutions such as Europol and Euro just work to enhance cooperation among member states, providing expertise and support in complex cross-border cases.

Challenges and Considerations

Extradition to the EU is not without challenges. Harmonizing legal systems, ensuring consistency in extradition procedures, and balancing the interests of justice are among the key challenges faced. Addressing these challenges requires continuous efforts to improve international legal frameworks and promote effective cooperation.

Recent Cases of Extradition from the European Union to India

In recent years, extradition has become an increasingly significant aspect of international cooperation, particularly between the European Union (EU) and India. This chapter explores notable cases of individuals being extradited from EU member states to India. It provides an analysis of these cases, shedding light on the legal, diplomatic, and practical aspects involved in the extradition process.

Overview of Extradition Agreements

Extradition from EU member states to India is typically facilitated through bilateral extradition agreements. These agreements outline the offenses for which extradition can be requested and the procedures to be followed, ensuring a legal and organized extradition process.

Recent Notable Cases

Case 1: Vijay Mallya

One of the most high-profile cases in recent times is the extradition of Vijay Mallya, an Indian businessman accused of financial irregularities and loan defaults. The extradition process involved lengthy legal battles, appeals, and diplomatic negotiations[160].

---

[160]   BBC News. "Vijay Mallya: India tycoon to learn extradition fate." BBC

Case 2: Nirav Modi

Another significant case is that of Nirav Modi, a diamond merchant accused in a major banking fraud case in India. His extradition involved complexities related to legal procedures and human rights concerns[161].

Case 3: Christian Michel

Christian Michel, an alleged middleman in the Agusta Westland VVIP chopper scam, was extradited from the UAE to India[162]. This case highlighted international cooperation in the fight against corruption and fraud.

Legal and Diplomatic Challenges

Extradition from the EU to India is not without challenges. Legal complexities, human rights considerations, and differences in legal systems pose hurdles in the smooth execution of extradition requests. Moreover, diplomatic efforts are often crucial in ensuring successful extraditions.

Future Prospects

Cooperation between the EU and India in the realm of extradition is expected to grow. Enhancements in legal frameworks, addressing challenges, and fostering strong diplomatic ties are essential for streamlining the process and ensuring timely and just extraditions.

INDIA'S RECENT SUCCESSES IN EXTRADITING FUGITIVES FROM THE UNITED KINGDOM

It is widely acknowledged that the Government of India ("GOI"), in the recent years, has taken a tougher stance against economic offenders fleeing to foreign jurisdictions to evade criminal prosecution and to enjoy the fruits of their crimes. The GOI has made concerted efforts to increase the number of countries with which it has extradition treaties including with Afghanistan, Lithuania, Malawi and Morocco.[163] The enforcement agencies such as the Central Bureau of Investigation and Enforcement Directorate have also been reinvigorated to pursue

---

[161]   The Guardian. (2023). "Nirav Modi's extradition case: what we know so far." The Guardian.

[162]   BBC News. "Christian Michel: The story so far." BBC.

[163]   Lok Sabha Unstarred Question No. 2528 - Extradition of Offenders: 26.12.2018

economic offenders to foreign shores through the mechanism of extradition.

Extradition is often a complex process and usually involves navigating the relevant extradition treaties or extradition arrangements, as well as the domestic laws of the country who receives the extradition request ("Requested State") from the country seeking extradition ("Requesting State") of the accused or convicted individual ("Requested Person"). India has extradition treaties with 50 countries and extradition arrangements with 11 countries.[164] Extradition treaties are bilateral treaties which provide a defined legal framework and obligates the contracting states to extradite to each other, individuals that are accused, charged with or convicted of extraditable offences. On the other hand, extradition arrangements are non-binding and do not carry legal obligations on the party states.[165]

More than 20 countries including the United Arab Emirates, Canada, United State of America and United Kingdom ("UK"). [166] At least 51 extradition requests by GOI are presently pending at various stages in different foreign jurisdictions.[167]

History of Extradition from UK to India:

Historically, India hasn't had an inspiring record when it comes to extraditing fugitives from the UK. India and the UK entered into an extradition treaty in 1992. However, between 1992 and 2016, India has successfully extradited only one individual from the UK: Mr. Samirbhai Vinubhai Patel who was extradited on 18 October 2016 in relation to the offence of murder.[168] In contrast, India has made at least 23 extradition requests to the UK during this period.[169]

However, recently, India has had some success in terms of the extradition proceedings against Mr. Sanjeev Chawla, accused of being

---

[164]   Rajya Sabha Unstarred Question No. 1164 - Extradition of Criminals: 28.11.2019

[165]   Aarshi Tirkey, "India's Challenges in Extraditing Fugitives from Foreign Countries", Issue Brief No. 270, November 2018, Observer Research Foundation.

[166]   https://mea.gov.in/emtsp.htm

[167]   Rajya Sabha Unstarred Question No. 1664 - Fugitive Economic Offenders

[168]   Rajya Sabha Unstarred Question No. 1164 - Extradition of Criminals: 28.11.2019

[169]   Lok Sabha Unstarred Question No. 2842- Extradition from UK: 02.08.2017.

involved in a match-fixing scandal and Mr. Vijay Mallya accused of being involved in a banking fraud. In light of the outcome of these two cases, India is certainly turning the tides and the warning bells may be ringing for those economic offenders who considered the UK a safe haven.

Legal Framework:

Extradition Treaty of 22 September 1992 ("Extradition Treaty") The Extradition Treaty between the UK and India was signed on 22 September 1992 and was ratified on 15 November 1993. It provides that both countries will extradite individuals who have committed 'extradition offences' which are constituted by conduct and which under the laws of both countries is punishable for at least one year. In other words, the UK will not extradite an individual to India unless that individual is accused of an offence that would be criminal under the laws of the UK as well as India and unless the offence is serious enough that it attracts a sentence of one year. These are common requirements - i.e. double criminality and minimum punishment - which are included in most extradition treaties. Notably, the Extradition Treaty does not preclude the extradition of its own nationals by either the UK or India.

The Extradition Treaty also provides certain exceptions where extradition may be refused including where (i) the offences are of a political character; (ii) the Requested Person can satisfy the Requested State that, his extradition is being sought for the purpose of prosecuting or punishing him on account of his race, religion, nationality or political opinions; or (iii) the offence carries the death penalty in the Requesting State, to name a few. Since extradition may be refused on these grounds, they are often incorporated in the defense of Requested Persons resisting extradition.

The Extradition Act, 2003 ("Extradition Act")

The Extradition Treaty provides the broad framework that governs the extradition between India and the UK. The relevant domestic UK law that governs extradition proceedings is the Extradition Act. The procedure provided under the Extradition Act differs depending on whether the Requesting State is a category 1 country (European Union member states) or category 2 country (other countries with which the UK has an extradition treaty). India is a category 2 country and therefore, Part 2 of the Extradition Act applies to extradition requests by India. As a category 2 country, an extradition request from India requires a decision from both the Secretary of State and the Court.

Procedure

In order to commence the extradition proceedings, the GOI must send an extradition request through the Ministry of External Affairs to the Home Office, UK. The extradition request must be accompanied by details of the Requested Person, details of the offence, authenticated copy of the arrest warrant issued against the Requested Person etc. If the Secretary of State, Home Office certifies the extradition request, the same is forwarded to the Westminster Magistrate Court ("Magistrate Court") designated to conduct all extradition proceedings for England and Wales.[170]

Thereafter, the Magistrate Court may issue a warrant for arrest of the Requested Person. The Requested Person is brought to the Magistrate Court and an extradition hearing is scheduled. Pursuant to the extradition hearing, if the Magistrate Court determines that all the procedural requirements have been satisfied, and there is no statutory bar to extradition, it must send the case back to the Secretary of State for a decision on whether to order extradition of the Requested Person. The Requested Person has a right to appeal the decision of the Magistrate Court to the High Court (with leave of the High Court). However, the High Court will not hear the appeal until the Secretary of State orders the Requested Person's extradition.[171]

The Secretary of State must extradite the Requested Person unless the same is prohibited under the Extradition Act for the reason that the Requested Person could face the death penalty, there is no specialty arrangement between the UK and the Requested State or the Requested Person was extradited to the UK from a third state (where the consent of the third state is required and such consent has been withheld). If no statutory prohibitions apply, the Secretary of State must order extradition within 2 months from the date he or she received the case. The Requested Person has the right to appeal

---

[170]   https://www.gov.uk/guidance/extradition-processes-and-review#extradition-from-the-uk- category-2-territories

[171]   Ibid

the decision of the Secretary of State to the High Court (with leave of the High Court). In case the Requested Person has filed an appeal against the Magistrate Court's decision, both appeals may be heard simultaneously by the High Court.[172]

The High Court's decision may be appealed to the Supreme Court

(subject to leave being granted by the High Court or the Supreme Court itself). Leave to appeal to the Supreme Court will only be granted in specific cases involving a point of law or public importance. Subject to any pending appeal, the Requested Person must be extradited within 28 days of the Secretary of State's decision to order extradition.[173]

Prima Facie Requirement

The prima facie requirement is not a prerequisite for European Union member states and category 2A territories. However, India is a category 2B territory, hence, in a case where the Requested Person has not been convicted, the Magistrate Court is required to decide whether there is enough admissible evidence to satisfy the prima facie test that there is a case to answer and that a trial of the Requested Person would be required had the offence taken place in the UK.[174] In order to determine whether there is a prima facie case, the Requesting State must identify the notional offence under the UK law which corresponds to the extradition offence for which the Requested Person's extradition is being sought by the Requesting State.

In deciding whether the Requested State has established a prima facie case, the Magistrate Court may consider various types of evidence including a statement made by a person in a document, if the statement is made to a police officer or someone charged with the duty of investigating offences or charging offenders, and if direct oral evidence by the person of the fact would be admissible.[175] The Magistrate Court will evaluate a number of factors while deciding whether a statement made in a document

---

172   Ibid.

173   Ibid

174   See Section 84(1) of the Extradition Act

175   See Section 84(2) of the Extradition Act

is admissible including the nature/source of the document, relevance of the evidence etc.[176] The issue of admissibility of evidence is often raised before the Magistrate Court as part of the Requested Person's defence.

Bars to Extradition

The Extradition Act bars the extradition of a Requested Person in certain circumstances, even if there is no corresponding bar under the Extradition Treaty. In the event that the Magistrate Court determines that any of the statutory bars to extradition apply, the Requested Person must be discharged. Consequently, these are often the grounds that are taken in the defence of Requested Persons. Some of the statutory bars to extradition include, amongst others, the following:

Double Jeopardy:

Where the Requested Person would be entitled to be discharged under any rule of law relating to previous acquittal or conviction assuming he was charged with the extradition offence in the part of the UK where the judge exercises his jurisdiction;[177]

Extraneous Considerations:

Where the extradition of the Requested Person is barred because (a) the request for his extradition is made for the purpose of prosecuting or punishing him on account of his race, religion, nationality, gender, sexual orientation or political opinions, or (b) if extradited the Requested Person might be prejudiced at his trial or punished, detained or restricted in his personal liberty by reason of his race, religion, nationality, gender, sexual orientation or political opinions;[178] and

Passage of Time:

Where it would be unjust or oppressive to extradite him by reason of the passage of time that has passed since the offence or since the person has been unlawfully at large.[179]

---

[176] See Section 84(3) of the Extradition Act

[177] See Section 80 of the Extradition Act .

[178] See Section 81 of the Extradition Act.

[179] See Section 82 of the Extradition Act.

Human Rights

While deciding whether a Requested Person may be extradited, the Magistrate Court must also consider whether or not extradition would be permissible in terms of the same not being in violation of the Requested Person's Convention Rights as defined under the Human Rights Act, 1988 (UK) ("Human Rights Act") which include the right to fair trial, prohibition of torture or degrading treatment etc. In case the Magistrate Court determines that the extradition of the Requested Person would result in a violation of these rights, then it cannot order the extradition.

Letters of Assurance

In the event that there is evidence that there is a real risk of impermissible treatment that bars the Requested Person's extradition, a Requesting State may overcome this hurdle by issuing a letter of assurance. Letters of assurances provide assurance that the Requested Person will not be exposed to such a risk and will be held in particular conditions, thus discounting the perceived risk. Such assurances are an important part of extradition law. While assessing the adequacy of a letter of assurance, the Magistrate Court may consider various factors such as

i. whether the assurances are specific or are general and vague;

ii. who has given the assurances and whether that person can bind the Requesting State; and

iii. whether compliance with the assurances can be objectively verified through diplomatic or other monitoring mechanisms.[180]

Since a letter of assurance is a diplomatic assurance provided by the Requesting State about the future of the Requested Person, the Requested State will also evaluate whether the Requesting State is a friendly country and whether it is governed by the rule of law where there is the expectation that the assurance given will be kept.

Sanjeev Chawla Case:

The GOI issued an extradition request dated 1 February 2016 seeking the extradition of Mr. Sanjeev Chawla for allegedly acting as a conduit between bookies who wanted to fix cricket matches and Hansie Cronje, the then captain of the South African test cricket team. It was the GOI's case that Mr. Sanjeev Chawla's conduct amounted to the offence of cheating under the Indian Penal Code ("IPC") and the nominal UK

---

[180]   See Barde vs Court of Florence [2014] EWHC 614 (Admin).

offence of 'conspiracy to give or agree to give corrupt payments in England and Wales".

One of the primary issues involved in this matter was the prison conditions of the Tihar Jail, New Delhi and whether the same would be a bar to Mr. Chawla's extradition as not being compatible with his right guaranteed by Article 3 of the Convention rights i.e. prohibition of torture and degrading treatment, as contended by Mr. Chawla. This objection was based on a report of Dr. Alan Mitchell on prison conditions, which contained findings of overcrowding, violence and lack of medical facilities. In response to this objection, the GOI provided two letters of assurance regarding the prison conditions.

The Magistrate Court only considered the first letter of assurance and decided that the same was inadequate as it was in general terms, and that the evidence established that there was a real risk of inhuman and degrading treatment to Mr. Chawla, which would violate his human rights. Therefore, the Court discharged Mr. Chawla. The GOI appealed the decision to the High Court. The High Court considered the second letter of assurance. However, it concluded that both the letters of assurance were inadequate and therefore "that there remains a real risk that if Mr Chawla is extradited and held at Tihar prison that he will be subjected to inhuman or degrading treatment contrary to article 3 of the ECHR". However, the High Court indicated that the GOI may rectify the situation by providing a more suitable assurance.

The GOI subsequently filed a third letter of assurance which, amongst other things, gave specific assurances that Mr. Chawla would be accommodated in a cell to be occupied exclusively by him, the wardwhere he would be lodged had inmates who had not violated any prison rules and were of satisfactory conduct and Mr. Chawla would be provided immediate medical attention if required, during his stay in the Delhi prisons. The High Court held that the information available about Tihar prisons and the terms of the third assurance were sufficient to show that there would be no real risk that Mr. Chawla would be subjected to impermissible treatment. Consequently, the High Court quashed the Magistrate Court's order discharging Mr. Chawla and directed the Magistrate Court to proceed as if Mr. Chawla had not been discharged.

Subsequently, the Magistrate Court sent the case to the Secretary of State for his decision. The Secretary of State approved the extradition. Mr. Chawla's application seeking leave to appeal was rejected by the High Court. After an attempt to move the European Court of Human Rights by Mr. Chawla failed, he was extradited to India in February 2020.

Vijay Mallya Case:

The GOI submitted an extradition request on 9 February 2017 seeking the extradition of Dr. Vijay Mallya in relation to his involvement in a banking fraud and for the commission of the offences of cheating and criminal conspiracy under the IPC read with offences under the Prevention of Corruption Act, 1988 and Prevention of Money Laundering Act, 2002 which corresponded to the notional UK offences of 'conspiracy to defraud', 'making false representations', 'diversion and dispersal of the proceeds of lending' and 'money laundering'.

In his defence, Dr. Mallya argued that the GOI failed to establish a prima facie case. Furthermore, he contended that his extradition was being sought for extraneous considerations, namely his political opinions. Dr. Mallya also argued that his extradition was barred since the same was not compatible with his Convention rights within the meaning of the Human Rights Act. Specifically, Dr. Mallya argued that there would be a risk to his right to a fair trial (Article 6) and prohibition of torture (Article 3). Dr. Mallya also made detailed arguments objecting to the admissibility of the GOI's evidence including witness statements under Section 161 of the Code of Criminal Procedure, 1973 ("CrPC"). Dr. Mallya relied upon the evidence of several experts including a report prepared by Dr. Alan Mitchell regarding prison conditions (this expert also provided evidence during Mr. Chawla' extradition hearing). For its part, aside from placing on record substantial evidence in support of its allegations, the GOI also gave a number of assurances regarding prison conditions.[181]

The Magistrate Court held that that there was a prima case that Dr. Mallya had committed the offence of conspiracy to defraud and conspiracy to launder money. It did not find any evidence to support Dr. Mallya's contention that his extradition was being sought for the purpose of prosecuting or punishing him on account of his political opinions. The Magistrate Court also accepted the assurances given by the GOI with respect to prison conditions and held that there were no grounds for believing that the Requested Person would face a real risk of being subjected to treatment contrary to Article 3. Likewise, it also held that there was no evidence that Dr. Mallya was at a real risk of suffering a flagrant denial of justice in terms of Article 6. Notably, the Magistrate Court held that the witness statements under Section 161 of the CrPC were admissible.

---

[181]   See Decision of Westminster Magistrates' Court in The Government of India vs. Vijay Mallya dated 10th December 2018.

Consequently, the case was sent to the Secretary of State for a decision to be taken on whether to order his extradition. The Secretary of State approved Dr. Mallya's extradition.

Dr. Mallya sought leave to file an appeal to the High Court against the decisions of the Magistrate Court and the Secretary of State under various grounds. Permission was refused on all grounds save one: the ground that the Magistrate Court was wrong to conclude that there was evidence "which would be sufficient to make a case requiring an answer by the person if the proceedings were the summary trial of an information against him".[182] The thrust of Dr. Mallya's defence was that the Magistrate Court had erred in determining that the prima facie test had been satisfied and in admitting the evidence filed by the GOI. The High Court rejected both contentions, it held that the Magistrate Court was correct in determining that there was a prima facie case and that the GOI's evidence, including the witness statements under Section 161 of the CrPC, were admissible. The appeal was dismissed on 20 April 2020.[183] Dr. Mallya's application seeking leave to file an appeal before the Supreme Court was dismissed on 14 May 2020. Consequently, unless Dr. Mallya is able to secure relief from the European Court of Human Rights, his extradition to India is now imminent.

Therefore, the successes of these two high profile extradition cases is a clear feather in the GOI's hat. Both these cases were vehemently contested by the concerned Requested Persons, and their respective defences made great efforts to prevent extradition. What emerges from these cases is that, when facing extradition to India, Requested Persons will commonly take up similar human rights and extraneous consideration arguments. In both these cases, the conditions of prisons in India was made a primary issue of the defence. However, the GOI has been able to dispel any perceived risk by giving adequate assurances. India ought to ensure that it lives up to its assurances so that the UK and other jurisdictions continue to have confidence that India will not breach assurances given by it. This may be important in case of future extradition cases. In light of these recent verdicts, the UK may no longer be a preferred destination for fugitive offenders from India. India's aggressive approach towards extradition undoubtedly is a deterrent and advances the principle that no one can escape the long arm of the law.

---

[182] See The Queen of the Application of Vijay Mallya vs Government of India & Ors [2019] EWHC 1849 (Admin).

[183] See The Vijay Mallya vs. Government of India & Ors [2020] EWHC 924 (Admin).

LIST OF THE FUGITIVES BROUGHT TO INDIA IN THE LAST FIVE YEARS

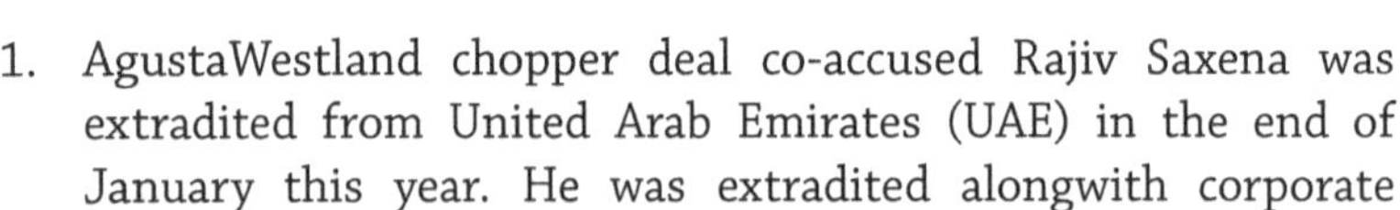

1. AgustaWestland chopper deal co-accused Rajiv Saxena was extradited from United Arab Emirates (UAE) in the end of January this year. He was extradited alongwith corporate lobbyist Deepak Talwar.

2. British national Christian Michel James was extradited from UAE on December 4, 2018 in a case of cheating and criminal conspiracy for his alleged role as middleman in AgustraWestland case.

3. Mohammed Yahya, who faces cases of cheating, forgery and criminal conspiracy, was extradited from Indonesia on October 12, 2018.

4. Vinay Mittal, who faces cases of cheating, forgery and criminal conspiracy, was extradited from Indonesia on September 9, 2018.

5. Mansoor/Farooq Takla, who faces charges of involvement in terrorist activities, was extradited from UAE on March 8, 2018.

6. Marinoiu Mohd Farooq Yasin, a Romanian national, was extradited from Nicaragua on March 3, 2018 in a bank fraud case.

7. Abubakr Kadir Lonut Alexandru was extradited from Singapore on September 23, 2017 in job scam racket case.

8. Abdul Raut Merchant Mohmmad Sultan was extradited from Bangladesh on November 8, 2016 on charges of murder.

9. Samirbhai Vinubhai Patel was extradited from Britain on October 19, 2016 on charges of murder, and criminal conspiracy.

10. Kumar Krushna Pillai was extradited from Singapore on June 27, 2016 in attempt to murder case.

11. Abdul Wahid Siddibapa was extradited from the UAE on May 20, 2016 for waging or attempt to wage war against India.

12. Willy Naruenartwanic, a Thai national, was extradited from Thailand on December 9, 2015 for waging or attempt to wage war against India.

13. Kollam Gangi Reddy was extradited from Mauritius on November 15, 2015 on charges of culpable homicide not amounting to murder, and attempt to murder.

14. Anup Chetia was extradited from Bangladesh on November 11, 2015 for waging or attempt to wage war against India.

15. Chhota Rajan was extradited from Indonesia on November 6, 2015 on charges of murder and kidnapping.

16. Bannaje Raja was extradited from Morocco on August 14, 2015 on charges of murder.

17. Jagtar Singh Tara was extradited from Thailand on January 16, 2015 on charges of murder.

BIBLIOGRAPHY

Books:

1.   P. Ramanatha Aiyar''s Concise Law Dictionary, Lexis Nexis, Fifth
   Edition

2.   Black's Law Dictionary, Centennial Edition (1891-1991), Sixth
   Edition

3.   J.G. Starke, *Introduction to International Law*, Tenth Edition
   Statutes:

1.   The Fugitive Offenders Act, 1881

2.   The Foreigners Act, 1946

3.   The Constitution of India, 1950

4.   The Indian Penal Code, 1860

5.   The Explosive Substances Act, 1908

6.   The Extradition Act, 1903

7.   The Extradition Act, 1962

8.   The Code of Criminal Procedure, 1973

9.   The Maharashtra Control of Organized Crimes Act, 1999

10.   The Narcotic Drugs and Psychotropic Substances Act, 1985

11.   The Unlawful Activities Prevention Act, 1967

12.   The Prevention of Terrorism Act, 2002

13.   The Anti-Hijacking Act, 1982

ABOUT AUTHOR

Dr. Anil Kumar Dixit

(M.A. in Political Science, LL.M., PGDJ and Ph.D.)

Professor & Principal, Career College of Law

Bhopal, (M.P)

Contact - akdagra@yahoo.co.in

Born in 1973 in the historic city of Agra, Uttar Pradesh, India, Dr. Anil Kumar Dixit has dedicated his life to the realms of law, education, and social activism. His educational journey began and concluded in Agra, where he earned his LLB, LLM, and a PhD in from Dr. Bhimrao Ambedkar University, following an MA in Political Science Subject.

With a profound passion for academia, Dr. Anil Kumar Dixit has accumulated rich teaching and research experience. Beyond the classroom, he engages with a wider audience through regular editorial contributions to newspapers and magazines. His articles delve into the intricate intersections of social, legal, and political issues. As, this is his fourth Book.

Dr. Anil Kumar Dixit has actively participated in numerous workshops, both national and international seminars, where he not only presented but also published thought-provoking research papers. His journey began in the world of journalism with the Hindi daily 'Aaj' in Agra, eventually ascending to the role of editor in various national newspapers over a span of 12 years.

Transitioning seamlessly between roles, Dr. Anil Kumar Dixit has served as an Assistant Professor, Associate, and Principal in Law College, Agra. Later, he embraced the position of Law Professor and

Research Dean at Maharishi Information Technology University in Lucknow. Presently, he holds the esteemed positions of Professor and Principal at Career College of Law, affiliated with Barkatullah University in Bhopal.

Dr. Anil Kumar Dixit is not only a distinguished academic but also a socially conscious individual actively engaged in the field of human rights protection and law. His contributions have been recognized with awards at different levels, and he has authored several impactful books that reflect his depth of knowledge and commitment to societal betterment.

THE END

www.ingramcontent.com/pod-product-compliance
Lightning Source LLC
LaVergne TN
LVHW092022190726
843493LV00002B/552